DESERT
AIR FORCE
AT WAR

DESERT AIR FORCE
AT WAR

CHAZ BOWYER &
CHRISTOPHER SHORES

LONDON

IAN ALLAN LTD

First published 1981

ISBN 0 7110 1154 0

© Chaz Bowyer and Christopher F. Shores 1981.

Published by Ian Allan Ltd, Shepperton, Surrey,
and printed by Ian Allan Printing Ltd at their works
at Coombelands in Runnymede, England.

Contents

Introduction

The Desert Air Force, and its illustrious forebears, are now one of the Royal Air Force's legends. A multi-national blending of air and ground crews, the DAF created a form of co-operative land/air warfare which ultimately was adopted by the Allied fighting services in every other theatre of the war in 1940-45, and proved to be the key to eventual victory. The path to that inter-Service integration of efforts was long and bloody; but with rare skill, stoic patience, outstanding courage, and no small sacrifice, the DAF won its laurels in superb fashion. Along that stony, weary pathway the individual members of the DAF also created a bond of comradeship with each other that withstood the harsh testing of deprivation and hazard, and living and working conditions which might have daunted lesser men.

The true heart of the DAF lay in its total dedication to the job – naught else assumed higher priority. Such mundane matters as parades, proper uniform, correct channels, and the many other inevitable facets of a peacetime-raised RAF bureaucracy were relegated to a level of mere incidental importance. It was an attitude reflected in the words of one of the DAF's most famous commanders, Arthur 'Maori' Coningham, who opined; 'Strip 'em of all non-essentials, give 'em plenty of work, and they'll be a happy lot.' Despite outward appearances – and the men of the DAF were ever easy to recognise in their highly individual interpretations of Service uniform – the men of the DAF were well disciplined. Not, it is true, in the mould of barrack-square fetishism, or the Uxbridge-mentality blind obedience to the printed regulation of T. E. Shaw's experience; but the willing, unenforced discipline of men

bonded in a common cause, sharing equally in a common peril.

The proving ground for the DAF were the northern territories of Africa bordering the Mediterranean Sea; an area virtually devoid of the more familiar facets of human occupation. Beyond a thin scattering of colonial towns, ports and villages, no great cities, industrial complexes, or suburban areas lay available for bloody devastation; only a vast, bald desert and endless acres of scrubland existed for the opposing forces to imprint with the pitiless hand of war. In direct contrast, during the latter years of the Mediterranean campaigns, the battlegrounds fought over throughout the length and breadth of Italy were an interlocking kaleidoscope of lush greenery, mountains, valleys, muddied plains, and a host of inhabited ancient towns and cities whose history stretched back to the beginnings of civilisation. That the men of the DAF coped with all the changing circumstances they encountered is in itself a tribute to their adaptability and wide flexibility in thought and deed.

Following the theme of all titles in this series, this book is not intended as any form of academic history of the Desert Air Force, but simply an evocation of the overall subject; an attempt to recapture something of the authentic contemporary atmosphere of the DAF during its relatively brief existence. It is no less a sincere, if small, tribute to all men of that elite, proud force. Equally, it is offered as a reminder of the many DAF men who did not live to witness the final victory; in the apt words of the memorial to the dead of Kohima, they '. . . gave our tomorrow for your today' – they must never be forgotten.

Apart from an obvious debt of gratitude owed to the various individual contributors herein, we wish to offer our sincere thanks to the many friends and acquaintances who gave prompt, unselfish help and advice during compilation. Listed alphabetically, these include particularly; R. C. B. 'Chris' Ashworth; Ray Aveyard; Vic Cashmore; Steven Challen; Wg Cdr A. G. Clennett; Peter Hepple; Ted Hine of the Imperial War Museum; G. Stuart Leslie; Dr F. T. Pearce; Mike Schoeman; Frank F. Smith; Dave Vincent; L. L. G. Willis; and the other private photograph owners who loaned their albums and prints. In addition we are indebted to Roland Stephens for his kind permission to use extracts from the diary of his brother Alwyn; to Robin A. Brown for permission to quote from his privately-published history of 112 Squadron; to J. A. Jones ('Jon') for permission to reproduce the 'Jon' cartoon; and, never least, to Dave Gray of Walkers Studios, Scarborough for his customary magic in deriving excellent prints for use in illustration from long-stored snaps and fading prints.

Chaz Bowyer: Norwich, 1980
Chris Shores: Hendon, 1980

Background

Above: **Stalwart of the opening months of various campaigns in the Middle East zones of war, the Gloster Gladiator proved itself to be a doughty fighter. This example, L8011, YK-O, of 80 Squadron's B Flight in 1940, is being flown by Flt Lt M. T. St J. Pattle, a South African and the RAF's highest-scoring fighter pilot throughout 1939-45./*AVM J. H. Lapsley***

The generic title Desert Air Force has been the subject of much misunderstanding and general presumption in the years since 1945. Therefore precise definition of what strictly comprised that now-legendary formation is necessary in order to clarify its roles, constitution, and not least thereby a succinct appraisal of its huge contribution to final victory over the Axis forces in what may loosely be termed the Middle East theatres of operations during the years 1940-45. The Desert Air Force (DAF) first formally came into existence late in 1941 under the initial title Western Desert Air Force (WDAF); a tactical command for direct aerial support of the British Eighth Army in North Africa. As such it was the RAF's first 'Tactical Air Force' – hence the later designation of the British and Commonwealth's main air support formation for the 1944 invasion of Europe as 2nd Tactical Air Force (2nd TAF). It was not until February 1943, after the vast deserts of Egypt and Libya had been left behind, that the title Desert Air Force truly applied, and then to a larger force which incorporated some of the air units which had been directly supporting the British 1st Army in Tunisia.

From that point on the DAF formed only a part of the far larger North-West (later, Mediterranean) Allied Tactical Air Force. Here it operated alongside the American-commanded XII Tactical Air Command and, later, also the Balkan Air Force. Primarily a fighter, fighter-bomber, and light bomber force, the DAF continued its prime role as support to the Eighth Army throughout the invasions of Sicily and Italy, the advance on Rome, and the ultimate battles across the northern Appenines and the north Italian plain.

Nevertheless, putting such pedantry aside, a rather wider interpretation of the DAF's ancestry and its first two years of operations should be taken if its eventual role and prowess are to be fully appreciated. On 10 June 1940, when war with Italy became a fact, the Royal Air Force presence in the Middle East had the larger part of its operational strength available for action over the Egyptian-Libyan border, and for protection of the main Royal Navy base at Alexandria, apart from protection of the vital Suez Canal sea-link to the Far East. The only element of this overall force which can be regarded truly

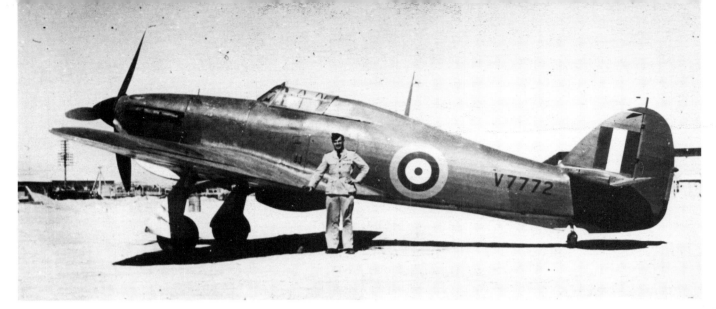

as the precursor of the DAF was the relative handful of Gloster Gladiators and Westland Lysanders based around the Sidi Barrani area for direct support of the resident army formations, but to provide a more balanced view the whole of No 202 Group, RAF – the operational arm of RAF, Middle East then – should be included up until the actual formation of the WDAF in October-November 1941. 202 Group, commanded by the Canadian Air Vice-Marshal Raymond Collishaw, in June 1940, comprised:

Squadron	Main base	Aircraft
30	Ismailia	Bristol Blenheim I
33	Qasaba	Gloster Gladiator
45	Helwan	Bristol Blenheim I
55	Fuka	Bristol Blenheim I
70	Heliopolis	Vickers Valentia
80	Amriya	Gloster Gladiator
112	Helwan	Gloster Gladiator
113	Ma'aten Bagush	Bristol Blenheim IV
208	Qasaba	Westland Lysander
211	El Daba	Bristol Blenheim I
216	Heliopolis	Bristol Bombay

Elsewhere throughout other areas of the Middle East were nine other squadrons; while the sole example of a Hawker Hurricane (L1669) was on the strength of 80 Squadron.

From the very beginning of hostilities the RAF undertook an aggressive, attacking role, striking at Italian Air Force forward airfields on the first day of war. Nevertheless, the British forces in Egypt were too weak to do more than frontier skirmishing, and when, in September 1940, Marshal Graziani's army advanced into Egypt, there was no alternative but to fall back. Fortunately, the Italian advance halted after only a few days and dug in. RAF squadrons continued to patrol offensively over the front lines, undertook reconnaissance and light bombing raids, and defended the Fleet at Alexandria. The decision to send air aid to the Greeks in November 1940 led to an immediate further

weakening of 202 Group, although a thin trickle of reinforcement Blenheims and Hurricanes began arriving from England, a few new squadrons began to join the Group or were formed locally. Then, early in December Gen Wavell, C-in-C, Middle East, launched a reconnaissance in strength under the command of Gen O'Connor across the Egyptian-Libyan border, with orders to exploit success. Supported by two squadrons of Hurricanes, one of Gauntlets and Gladiators, the Blenheim squadrons not despatched to Greece, and by heavy bombers from the Nile Delta area (Wellingtons), this reconnaissance rapidly developed into a major offensive.

The demoralised, ill-equipped, and badly organised Italian colonial army was chased right across Cyrenaica by a substantially smaller force, and the Italian Air Force was severely mauled – particularly on the ground at its airfields. The ports of Tobruk, Bardia and Benghazi were taken, and the victorious British were on the borders of Tripolitania when, from sheer exhaustion and over-stretched lines of supply and communication, they necessarily halted their headlong

Top: **Hurricanes first began to arrive in small quantities in the Middle East from June 1940, and the first fully-equipped unit was 274 Squadron at Amriyah. This example, V7772, belonged to 3 Squadron RAAF in March 1941, when it is pictured at Amriyah with its pilot Fg Off Alan Rawlinson.**/*via F. F. Smith*

Above: **Part-view of Amriyah in March 1941, with a 3 Sqn RAAF Hurricane in foreground, P3822 'Pamela', flown by Flt Lt B. R. Pelly (later, Gp Capt, OBE).**/*via F. F. Smith*

Above: **Fiat CR42** *after combat . . .*

Right: **Early Luftwaffe fighter units in North Africa were part-equipped with the Messerschmitt Bf109E variant; as in this case of I/JG27, being flown by Leutnant Werner Schroer, one of the most successful German pilots in the subsequent campaign.**
/G. W. Joos

advance. Just at that point further withdrawals of RAF and Army units to Greece took place on direct orders from London, despite protests by on-the-spot commanders – at the very time when the first German elements were arriving in Tripoli to bolster the retreating Italian forces. Late in March 1941 a highly mobile German-Italian force commanded by Gen Erwin Rommel hit back at the much-weakened British line, which collapsed almost at once and in quick time was rolled steadily back into Egypt, leaving only the besieged port of Tobruk in Allied hands. It was one of the lowest points in the fortunes of the war for the British, as German forces also poured into Yugoslavia and Greece. By

fortunate coincidence, however, the campaign against the Italians in East Africa had just been concluded successfully, thereby releasing many ground and air units from East Africa and Aden for addition to Allied forces in Egypt. At the same period a major sea convoy from England furnished fresh tanks and new Hurricanes. Rommel's forces had also been exhausted by their rapid drive to Egypt, with over-extended lines of resupply complicated by the dogged resistance of the Allied defenders of Tobruk, and the ground war became momentarily static.

The fall of Greece and Crete, though a bloody tragedy, brought back to the Egyptian 'fold' the remnants of all surviving squadrons originally sent there, and permitted their re-equipment, partly from the initial major deliveries of new American aircraft, Curtiss P-40 Tomahawks and Martin Marylands. Yet another diversion of strength came in May 1941 with the rebellion in Iraq, followed by the desirability of occupying a hostile, Vichy French-dominated Syria during June. In the meantime, in mid-June 1941, an Allied offensive, code-named 'Battleaxe', was launched against Rommel, and this was supported by the first South African Air Force (SAAF) squadrons to reach Egypt, and by the first Tomahawks and Marylands to go into action in the area. Total air strength available for this 'push' included five squadrons of fighters, six of light-medium bombers, one squadron of tactical reconnaissance (Tac-R) Hurricanes, plus the heavy bombing support of the Delta-based Wellingtons. Yet the outcome was a minor disaster; no territory was gained, while the three days of heavy fighting produced large losses in Allied tanks and aircraft.

During the subsequent period of virtual stalemate both sides strove to rebuild their forces; the Axis with a view to capturing Tobruk, a vital resupply port, and then eventual capture of the Suez Canal zone. With Hitler's ill-fated invasion of Russia now under way, Rommel's forces were part-denied essential supplies and were thus in a rather worse position than the Allies for any such build-up of strength. At this period 202 Group received a fresh commander, AVM Sir Arthur 'Maori' Coningham, and the first steps were taken in forming a true tactical air force – which eventually led to the true DAF. During July 1941 the first wing, No 253, was formed experimentally for close support roles, and included two squadrons of Hurricanes and one of Blenheims – the latter with additional forward armament for a ground-strafing role. Shortly after, three fighter wings were freshly formed; 258 and 269 which were initially tasked with operations over the front line, and 262 which was responsible for defence of the Nile Delta zone. The two former wings were to form the nucleus of WDAF.

By the beginning of November 1941 both sides were nearing readiness states for new land offensives, but the British and

Below: **Blenheim IVs played a not insignificant part in the first years of the desert campaigns, particularly during Operation 'Crusader' when seven squadrons and a detachment were used. Nearest aircraft (Z5893) displays its under-nose, rear-firing machine gun for tail defence.**/*IWM*

Bottom: **Synonymous in many people's minds with the DAF was the Curtiss Kittyhawk, especially the Sharkmouth marking so aptly applied to the aircraft of 112 Squadron RAF.**/*IWM*

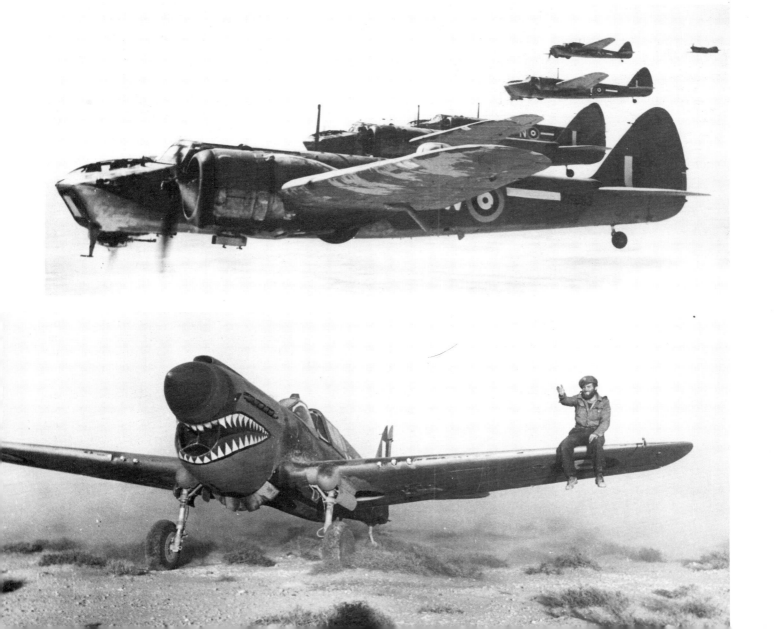

Top: **Against the Messerschmitt Bf109F, the DAF's Hurricanes were often at a disadvantage in the context of overall performance. This victim behind German lines was 94 Squadron's FZ-P.**/*F. Selinger*

Above: **Be it ever so 'umble . . . typical 'bivvy' residence for all ranks of the DAF throughout the North African battles.**/*IWM*

Commonwealth forces struck first; launching 'Crusader' on 18 November. In support in the air was a total of 28 squadrons overall. Of these 258 Wing had four Hurricane and two Tomahawk squadrons; 262 Wing had three Tomahawk, two Hurricane fighter squadrons, and 80 Squadron with the first Hurri-bombers. 269 Wing defended the rear areas with two RAF Hurricane squadrons and a composite, attached Fleet Air Arm unit formed from Hurricanes and Grumman Martlets. In addition were six Blenheim IV units, two with Marylands, one with Douglas Bostons, one flying Beaufighters, one of Blenheim ground-strafers, and two Maryland general reconnaissance squadrons. Behind them came two strategic recce units, plus five squadrons of heavy night bombers. It meant that for the first time the RAF was numerically at least equal to the Axis air forces, and a measure of air superiority was established during the subsequent two months of fierce fighting, albeit with losses on both

sides at a high level. The result was that the Axis forces were compelled to withdraw westwards, Tobruk was relieved, and by mid-April 1942 the Allies had regained all the ground lost a year before. January 1942 also saw the operational debut of the new Curtiss Kittyhawk as WDAF's main air superiority fighter.

Almost at once Rommel launched a counter-attack, pushing the Allied armies back as far as the Gazala line, halfway across the Cyrenaican bulge, and yet another period of dual recoupment began. At this time the outbreak of war with Japan led to the withdrawal of several units, air and ground, from the Middle East for service in the Far East, but – more significantly – diverted badly-needed reinforcements for the North African struggle.

Following 'Crusader', all Blenheims were officially taken off day operations and reverted to night bombing forays only, or were replaced by modern American designs. Complete reorganisation of the WDAF followed in March 1942. 211 Group was created to control all units on the Libyan front, while 202 Group continued to administer the many base and Delta area units. 258 and 262 Wings became re-labelled as 243 and 239 Wings respectively, while a new 233 Wing was formed. The two Tac-R units in 211 Group were fully equipped with fighter aircraft, while Baltimores now re-equipped two RAF and one SAAF squadrons, and the Hurricane IID, armed with 40mm anti-tank cannons was introduced. At that same time the first squadron of Spitfire Vs began operations over the desert, and a Hurricane unit commenced a night intruder role.

By late May 1942 both opposing land forces were poised to resume the offensive, but Rommel struck first, opening a long slogging battle of attrition which eventually broke the

Top: **Curtiss Tomahawks of 3 Squadron RAAF on patrol during the side-show Syrian campaign, above typical desert scenery.**/*IWM*

Above: **The Vickers Wellington – universally nicknamed 'Wimpy' – was another stalwart of the bomber back-up operations in North Africa. This example is believed to have been a 38 Squadron machine.**

Left: **True heavy bombers for Middle East operations were part-represented by the Liberators used by 108 Squadron RAF. In this view of AL574, the tail gunner, Sgt G. W. S. Challen, demonstrates the home-made defence 'system' first applied – two .300-inch machine guns on a light alloy tripod, hand-operated. Later, sliding doors were added to the 'turret'.**/*G. W. S. Challen*

13

14

Allied lines after suffering profuse tank losses in the El Adem area. WDAF itself was in a position of numerical, if not technical superiority to the Luftwaffe and Italian air forces; and now as never before the squadrons were thrown into the attack against Rommel's advancing Afrika Korps; particular attention being paid to the Axis supply convoys, while the medium bombers went out in impeccable 'boxes' of at least 18 at a time to attack troop concentrations and similar targets often several times each day. Until then, ground-attacks had been limited to strafing with guns, with occasional 40lb or even 250lb bombs being carried by the sturdy Hurricanes. Tomahawks had no intrinsic provision for bomb-carrying, and when the Kittyhawks first appeared their initial task was as fighter cover and escort for the bombers. The Kittyhawks quickly proved themselves to be excellent fighter-bombers, capable of lifting 250lb or 500lb bombs, even 1000lb later. As the Spitfire gradually assumed the air superiority role, the Kittyhawks concentrated more and more on their new fighter-bomber activities; a duty of increasing importance to the land war.

WDAF by then was well versed in the rapid fluctuations of the ground battle, and its squadrons were fully mobile for the 'leapfrogging' tactics of unceasing support to the army; able to operate effectively from any fresh landing ground within 24 hours if required. In June, when the Eighth Army was forced into a hasty retreat from the Gazala position, the WDAF squadrons were fiercely active in support, and deserve much of the credit for preventing the orderly retreat becoming an all-out rout; thereby enabling the Eighth Army to reach prepared positions at El Alamein as an army in being, with the bulk of its equipment intact. Allied air losses to the German fighter force mounted alarmingly, yet rarely did the WDAF fail to reach its targets and its pilots often nullified Luftwaffe attempts to reach theirs. As the Eighth Army consolidated their position at El Alamein, beating off attempts to dislodge them with the ever-ready aid of WDAF, the equipment of the air units was up-dated, and the first American squadrons joined their command; one fighter and one bomber group with P-40F Warhawks and B-25 Mitchells respectively. Meanwhile the bulk of the other RAF Middle

Above left: **Hurricane IIDs, fitted with two 40mm under-wing cannons, proved highly effective against Rommel's panzers. This example belonged to 6 Squadron RAF, while under training at Shandur, 1942.**

Left: **Curtiss Tomahawk AN325, 'W', of 3 Squadron RAAF, 1941.**/*RAAF*

Right: **Worthy opponent. Macchi 202 of 91 Squadriglia, 10 Gruppo, 4 Stormo** *(Baracca),* **pictured in May 1942.**/*Stato Maggiore Aeronautica*

Below: **An American design of light bomber prominent in the desert air war was the Douglas Boston; exemplified here by AL755, B-Baker of 114 Squadron RAF, based at Canrobert in April 1943, and being flown by Fg Off Gellatly RNZAF.**

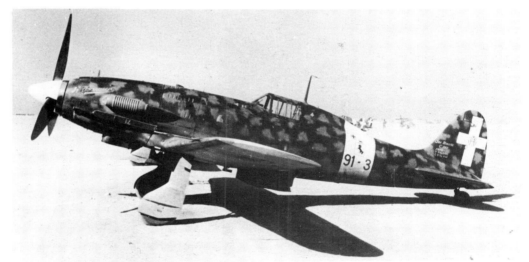

Above: **14 Squadron RAF, a veteran Middle East unit, received Martin Marauders late in 1942; one of its earliest machines being FK375, 'D', named** *Dominion Revenge* **seen here.**/*IWM*

Left: **The introduction of Spitfires to North Africa, suitably modified for desert conditions, came in 1942, when the first fully-equipped unit, 145 Squadron RAF, commenced Spitfire operations in June. Here one of the unit's aircraft, ER228, ZX-S warms up prior to take-off.**/*N. L. R. Franks*

Below: **Mercy angel. De Havilland 86a of No 1 Air Ambulance Unit, RAAF. This unit arrived in Egypt in July 1941 and began western desert duties in October that year.**/*IWM*

East strength received a higher proportion of fresh combat units for coastal, night strategic bombing, and defence roles. By the eve of the great battle of El Alamein – 24 October – WDAF had increased to two groups. Under WDAF HQ's direct command were an air ambulance squadron, 3 SAAF Wing, 232 Wing, the 12th Bombardment Group, USAAF, 285 Recce Wing, 211 Group with Hurricane IIDs, 233 and 239 Wings with eight squadrons of Kittyhawks and Tomahawks, the USAAF's 57th Fighter Group, and 244 Wing with Spitfires and Hurricane night intruders. Backing this force were 7 SAAF and 243 Wings with eight Hurricane squadrons, lumped under the aegis of 212 Group.

As the Eighth Army moved westward following its victory at El Alamein, only 211 Group moved forward at first in support, though the bomber squadrons maintained their efforts over the retreating Axis columns as long as these remained in attack range, and not until January 1943 did the bomber wings move westwards to join in renewed operations as the Allied advance halted just short of Tripoli. 212 Group was then transferred to HQ Air Defence, Eastern Mediterranean, remaining in Egypt and Cyrenaica, leaving a much leaner WDAF to continue forward with the Eighth Army. By the end of January 1943 Tripoli had been taken and the first moves into southern Tunisia were made. By then 211 Group had been reinforced with a further USAAF Warhawk Group, while 244 Wing had received two more Spitfire squadrons, one SAAF and one RCAF.

On 18 February 1943 came a total reorganisation of Allied air forces in the Mediterranean area, including all units of the WDAF, RAF Middle East, Malta, Tunisia and Algeria. The new command was titled North-West African Allied Air Force, with a number of subsidiary commands beneath its new banner; one of these being the NW African Allied Tactical Air Force, commanded by WDAF's Air Marshal Coningham. Of the four subordinate formations within Coningham's force, one was the Desert Air Force, as WDAF now became retitled, with Air Vice-Marshal Harry Broadhurst as its latest commander, which relinquished all its former light and medium bombers to a newly-formed Tactical Bomber Force with the NWAATAF.

As operations continued, on 26 March 1943 came the first major use of fighter-bombers in a land battle. The Eighth Army's frontal attack on the Mareth Line in southern Tunisia had been held, but a New Zealand out-flanking movement through the Tebaga Gap was proposed – a natural break in the hill-line guarding Tunisia from the south which was heavily defended by Axis forces.

Late that afternoon, following an artillery bombardment, two waves of Kittyhawks and Warhawks from 233,239 Wings and two USAAF groups swept in and devastated the anti-tank gun emplacements as the New Zealand Division moved forward. Losses to ground fire were heavy, but the objective was achieved, and the assaulting infantry and tanks pierced the gap with minimal casualties. Operations then resumed a 'normal' pattern of chasing a retreating foe up the coastal roads of southern and central Tunisia. In April much attention was paid to the varied attempts to reinforce, or evacuate, German and Italian units commanded by Field Marshal von Arnim, Rommel's successor. One such ploy was to despatch huge formations of Luftwaffe transport aircraft from Italy, and these massive gaggles were eagerly sought by the DAF fighters. Perhaps the peak of such engagements came on 18 April, when the 57th

Below: **Named** *Wings of Mercy,* **this Fairchild 91, HK832, originally with Panair do Brasil, was acquired by British-American Ambulance Corps, and delivered to the ASR Flight on 25 November 1941. Used along the north African coastline, it eventually hit a floating object off Benghasi on 17 May 1943 and sank.**

Fighter Group, USAAF claimed a total of 59 Junkers Ju 52/3s, together with 14 escorting fighters in a single massive combat over the Cap Bon area – a victory thereafter referred to as the 'Palm Sunday Massacre'. Next day Kittyhawks of 7 SAAF Wing (the latest title for the former 233 Wing) claimed 22 more German transports, while on 22 April the same SAAF Wing claimed the complete destruction of a 20-aircraft formation of the mammoth Messerschmitt Me 323 six-engined troop conveyors.

When the war in Africa finally ceased with the surrender of the remaining Axis troops on 13 May 1943, the DAF was quite a small part of the overall Allied air force in the Middle East, yet remained the force's prime cutting edge, receiving the best equipment and remaining in the forefront of events. Though deprived of the Hurricane IID 'can-openers', and – temporarily – 7 SAAF Wing as it replaced its Kittyhawks with Spitfire Vs; DAF was now given two Wings of Spitfire Vs and IXs. These 10 squadrons, together with 239 and 244 Wings, two USAAF groups of P-40Fs, and the recce units, completed the contemporary strength of DAF, which moved to Malta in June and July ready for the projected invasion of Sicily. The latter, code-named Operation 'Husky', commenced on 10 July with the DAF pilots providing faithful cover for 'their' Eighth Army's contribution to the landings in the eastern half of the island. After the initial heavy air combat over the beaches, however, few Axis aircraft were seen, and the latter stages of the battles saw DAF fighters again savaging Axis air trooper formations.

With Sicily secured by mid-August, the Eighth Army began its invasion of the Italian mainland by crossing to the southern tip of Italy on 3 September, and six days later the Anglo-American Fifth Army stormed ashore further north at Salerno, just south of Naples.

Left: **Engine maintenance in the desert – the hard way!**

Below: **NAAFI Up! Spitfires of 601 Squadron provide a backdrop to the arrival of the ubiquitous 'NAAFI Wagon'.**/*IWM*

By the end of that month both armies had joined up, and began an advance up the western side of the peninsula by the 5th, and up the eastern side by the Eighth Army. In October airfields were occupied on the Foggia Plain, where the DAF received back a number of its former bomber squadrons with 3 SAAF Wing and 232 Wing. 7 SAAF Wing's Spitfires also rejoined the DAF, a third SAAF Spitfire squadron was added, and 5 SAAF Squadron, the only remaining Kittyhawk unit, was transferred to 239 Wing. DAF was by now at its peak strength, but it was to be short-lived. Two squadrons of 322 Wing were sent to the Far East, while the rest of the wing, plus a squadron from 324 Wing, were sent to Syria.

As the harsh Italian winter set in the Eighth Army crossed the Trigno and Sangro rivers, with the DAF in its customary support roles, and a new, sophisticated form of close support system was introduced – the 'Rover David' and 'Cab Rank'. These involved maintaining formations of patrolling fighter-bombers overhead able to be called down immediately by RAF liaison officers with the forward infantry onto pin-pointed targets and obstacles in the path of the advancing army. These tactics were later to be employed with equal

Above: **Marauder 'M-Mother' of 12 Squadron SAAF over Acona harbour.**/*SAAF*

Right: **Mustang IVs of 3 Squadron RAAF over Italy, early 1945. Nearest, KH583, CV-K, was being flown by Flt Lt Ken Richards.**/*via F. F. Smith*

Below: **Wing Leader. Lt-Colonel L. Wilmot, SAAF of 239 Wing, DAF taxies in his personally-initialled Mustang III in early 1944, Italy.**/*Dr F. T. Pearce*

success after the invasion of Normandy in June 1944 by aircraft of the 2nd TAF. This latter invasion was responsible for the withdrawal of most of the top echelon of officers on DAF's staff when Coningham, Broadhurst et al returned to England and joined 2nd TAF, where their vast desert experience of air-to-ground co-operation was to be employed with great success. In their place the DAF received its latest commander, AVM William Dickson.

On 22 July 1944 came the seaborne invasion at Anzio, and as part-aid to this venture DAF was partly moved westward. It lost the services of one USAAF group at this time, while the other US group, now converted to P-47 Thunderbolts, left in the late spring for Corsica; leaving the DAF with no USAAF elements for the first time in the past 18 months. It was not to be until May that German resistance to the Allied armies was at last pierced to permit the Allies to sweep forward into Rome; but during that early part of 1944 much of the DAF's efforts had been extended to assisting Marshal Tito's partisans in Yugoslavia. New aircraft types had also begun arriving, with 3 SAAF Wing receiving Martin Marauders, and 239 Wing gradually

re-equipping several squadrons with Mustang III fighters; the latter having very long range capability and able to lift up to 2000lb of bombs. In view of these fresh designs, DAF's Bostons and Baltimores were now used mainly for night interdiction sorties against the enemy's road and rail communications.

Following the fall of Rome, many American units were then withdrawn from the Italian scene to join the forces about to invade southern France; leaving the DAF responsible for the whole of the much-weakened Italian front at a time when a major assault was about to tackle the strongly-held Gothic Line. To bridge the gaps, more units were sent to the DAF from Egypt, and a new wing, 253, was formed, plus four new Baltimore squadrons which joined 3 SAAF Wing for day bombing duties. In the event a lack of opposition to the invasion of Southern France permitted many units to be returned to Italy during September-October 1944. A combination of the fall of Rome and, particularly, the Allied invasion of Normandy, caused the withdrawal of virtually all Luftwaffe units in Italy, and the lack of air opposition gave the Spitfire IX squadrons free rein to undertake fighter-bomber sorties by the autumn, being joined in

Left: **Among the mountains, 225 Squadron RAF's Spitfires lined up at Florence in April 1945.**

Below: **Fully war-loaded Spitfire of 2 Squadron SAAF over the Sangro River, Italy in late 1944.**/*via T. Hooton*

this role eventually by the much-praised Spitfire VIIIs with which 244 Wing was equipped. The only active Luftwaffe now came by night, and here the local Mosquito and Beaufighter night defenders found plentiful victims.

The cruel Italian winter of 1944-45 nullified operations on the ground to great extent, and it was not until the spring of 1945 that the Allied armies could launch any meaningful offensive. In the interim the air forces concentrated on interdiction sorties against communications targets across the north Italian Plain as far north as the Brenner Pass. Then, in April, came the final Allied offensive, covered by massive air support, and enemy resistance melted away. On 24 April an armistice was signed, and on 2 May all fighting in Italy officially ceased. The long hard road from the bald deserts of Africa and Tunisia, across the Mediterranean, into Sicily, and ultimately the long, bitterly contested slog up the entire length of Italy had culminated in an unequivocal triumph. The sands of Egypt and Libya had been the breeding ground for a supremely successful Allied air-ground partnership, from which matured a fighting combination of arms which proved unconquerable; not only in the Mediterranean zones but, later, in Europe and the dank jungles of Burma. Exemplifying that unbeatable inter-Service brotherhood was the Desert Air Force and its illustrious forebears – a cohesive amalgam of air crews, ground crews and aircraft which epitomised the essence of true air power.

Left: **The air assault on Monte Cassino on 15 March 1944 was maintained by waves of Allied bombers at 15-minute intervals from 0830 to 1430 hrs that day. Here, one wave of Mitchells from the 488th BS,340th BG of the USAAF's 12th AF wings its way towards the target.**/*USAAF*

Below: **Salute. DAF Spitfires in the mass victory flypast on May 1945 over Campoformido airfield, Italy.**/*IWM*

Blenheim Nav

When, in April 1941, the Allied campaign in Italian East Africa was successfully concluded, a number of squadrons became available for service in the Western Desert. Among the first to arrive in Egypt was 14 Squadron, a Blenheim IV bomber unit, one of whose navigators was Geoffrey Whittard. Later he became the squadron's senior navigator, flying usually with the squadron commander, and was eventually promoted to flight commander, despite not being a pilot. The squadron's arrival in Egypt at a time when British forces in the desert were very much on the defensive, and Tobruk was under Axis siege, at first proved somewhat traumatic:

'When the squadron arrived at Heliopolis from Port Sudan on 9 April 1941, with instructions to spend the next three weeks re-equipping and training prior to proceeding to the Western Desert, we all realised that, although the previous few months had been quite active operationally, the circumstances under which we had been living and flying bore scant resemblance to those we could expect to meet in the desert. We had been based at Port Sudan Airport and although the town of Port Sudan itself offered little in the way of entertainment, we were not totally confined to Service surroundings during off-duty hours. The officers had been living in the Red Sea Hotel until latterly, when a school was taken over and converted to an extremely comfortable mess. Actual operations had been varied, on Wellesleys at first, then Blenheim IVs from October 1940, often co-operating with the Army by bombing enemy positions around the area, but mainly attacking aerodrome hangars, factories, railways, harbour installations and shipping, together with occasional anti-submarine patrols and general reconnaissance work. Our escorts, when practicable, were provided by Gloster Gladiators, and enemy aircraft encountered were usually Fiat CR32s and CR42s. The ack-ack, whilst severe over main targets was otherwise not a great problem. Our casualties were fortunately comparatively few considering the number of sorties flown.

Below: **Bombing up a 114 Squadron RAF Blenheim V in 1942.**

'The first sortie into the Western Desert by 14 Squadron provided a rude awakening and immediately brought home to us the fact that conditions in future were going to be vastly different to those we had experienced during the Eritrean campaign. So when, on 13 April – only four days later than our arrival at Heliopolis – one of two aircraft ordered to fly up to the desert was shot down, we realised fully that we were entering a sphere where very different conditions would be met, and different tactics would be needed. Our orders were to fly to Maaten Bagush, land there and receive further instructions, which turned out to be to proceed to the Tobruk area and carry out a reconnaissance, then land at Tobruk with our reports. It was impressed upon us how vital it was to approach Tobruk airfield along a specific corridor, and our flight to Bagush had already shown us that a specialised form of navigation was necessary over the desert with its few landmarks to assist in location of definite spots. Whether it was inexperience in this respect which led to the loss of the other aircraft we were never sure, but ack-ack and fighter activity along the corridor was very considerable. Plt Off Ormiston, a very competent Rhodesian pilot, and his navigator, and wireless operator/air gunner, both equally capable, were flying some way behind us – we'd been instructed not to fly too close together – and it was impossible to be certain whether they were shot down by one of the several Messerschmitt Bf110s which were around or, if they had not been exactly within the corridor, by our own ack-ack.

'Although 14 Squadron's operations were reasonably varied, the nature of the terrain over which the desert war was being fought did tend to limit somewhat the type of work we normally carried out. Most of our daytime targets were troop concentrations and

Above: **14 Squadron crews, including Geoffrey Whittard (far right) and 'Buck' Buchanan (second from left).**/*G. Whittard*

Right: **113 Squadron RAF's Blenheims setting out, 1941.**/*S. W. Lee*

movements of MT and tanks, which we bombed and sometimes ground-strafed; whilst at night they tended to be mainly landing grounds on which we dropped bombs and spikes, in addition to bombing parked aircraft. All such trips were mainly of comparatively short duration because we usually operated from ALGs (Advanced Landing Grounds) to be as near the targets as possible. It came as rather a surprise, therefore, when on 23 May 1941 we were ordered to attack Maleme landing ground in Crete, in daylight. We welcomed the change of target which would entail a flight duration of more than five hours, leaving little reserve on our Blenheims' maximum range; and as the majority of the flight would be over the sea, other factors, especially on the navigation side, would have to be calculated from a new angle. Several of these trips were made with formations of five or six aircraft, causing considerable damage to the airfield, aircraft and other surrounding targets. Unfortunately, our losses were rather heavy. After a few days we reverted to our normal desert operations and it was not until April 1942 that we again attacked targets in Crete – and then by night.

'It was amazing how in the desert, with no outside attractions and life confined to such a small area with conditions at times very primitive, there was such a great spirit of co-operation everywhere. We had people from nearly all walks of life amongst the regular personnel, the pre-war Volunteer Reservists, and the wartime entrants who made up 14 Squadron at various times, and all worked efficiently together without any prejudices. No doubt a great deal of the credit for such a spirit existing was due to the excellent leadership and example set by two of the squadron's most famous commanding officers, Wg Cdr (later, Air Vice-Marshal) Deryck Stapleton, and his successor Wg Cdr J. K. Buchanan. "Buck" stayed with 14 Squadron until May 1942, having taken over command from Deryck Stapleton in November 1941. Although both were regarded as excellent squadron commanders, they were very different characters in many ways. Deryck was of a more serious nature and possessed exceptional administrative qualities, highly capable in all fields, but less spectacular than Buck. He adhered to the text book more than Buck and although on the surface *appearing* less adventurous, displayed all the necessary daring and courage when required, as shown, for merely one example, on 26 November 1940, when he landed in enemy territory on the way back from a bombing raid to rescue the crew of one of our aircraft which had been shot down when we were intercepted by enemy fighters. 14 Squadron was indeed very fortunate to have

Left: **Bombing MT and tanks south-west of Sollum on 17 June 1941, pilot J. K. Buchanan, and navigator/bomb aimer, Geoffrey Whittard.**/*G. Whittard*

25

two such outstandingly competent successive commanders, and both were very popular with all who served under them, especially their respective crews, none of whom could have wished to fly with better pilots or captains.

'Buchanan's appearance itself was disconcerting – at first. He was of slight build, seemed to be immaculately dressed and groomed in spite of only being in khaki shorts and shirt, and he spoke with a fairly quiet but aristocratic voice, and generally did not give the impression of being a tough, dare-devil type. It was obvious to us all from the first day he joined the squadron that his main love and interest in life was flying. He was a natural pilot and enjoyed every minute he could spend in the air, no matter what the duty. He would never miss a single opportunity of flying on an operational sortie, or if that was not possible, of air testing or organising a training flight either for his own benefit or that of his crew.

'On 13 January 1942, whilst we were based with three other Blenheim squadrons at Gambut, there arrived Morley Lister, an American female press officer who had flown in from Cairo to gather material for *Life* magazine. As soon as Buck was introduced to her it was obvious they were going to get on well together; she must have fallen for his charm on the spot, and before long he had promised to take her on a bombing trip ordered for that same afternoon. It was a short flight, lasting only an hour, as the target – enemy transport and tanks at Halfaya Pass – was not far away. After landing it was decided that Morley should tell the captain of the aircraft which had brought her from Cairo to return without her, as she had "more research" to do . . . So she stayed on as

Buck's guest, the only female in the desert at that time except, perhaps, for a few nurses at Mersa Matruh area. She was with us for ten days in all, during which time Buck took her on a longer trip lasting five hours overall on 22 January, which entailed leading a formation of nine aircraft to Msus for briefing, picking up our fighter escort, then on to bomb MT and tanks along the Agedabia – El Agheila road. Morley was forced to return to Cairo next day by a very strongly worded and threatening signal received from her HQ.

'It was only after considerable argument and opposition from Buck that he was forced to accept an HQ appointment in April 1942, but we were not surprised to learn that his powers of persuasion very soon enabled him to talk his way back to operations, after only a few months of duty at HQ. We were later extremely sad to learn that he was eventually shot down over the Mediterranean Sea in a Beaufighter, and were incensed to read in a report of his death that it was alleged he had boasted that "No German pilot is good enough to shoot me down". Buck *never* boasted – he didn't need to. He merely had great confidence and faith in himself, his aircraft, and his comrades. Considering his many achievements, he was the most modest of men, and never talked of his deeds.*

* Wg Cdr J. K. Buchanan DSO, DFC, Croix de Guerre, had flown some 230 sorties over 13 different countries when he left 14 Squadron. From November 1942 he commanded 272 Squadron's Beaufighters in Malta, claimed at least 11 victories, then commanded 227 Squadron in 1943. In December 1943 his aircraft was shot down by flak during a raid across the Aegean, he ditched during the return flight, and was last seen astride a floating petrol tank in obvious good spirits. It was, however, several days before he was found, by which time he had died in his dinghy from dehydration and exposure.

Left: **Part-cynical portrayal of the 'multi-role' duties expected of 113 Squadron RAF's Blenheim crews in 1941-42.**

Below: **Blenheim I, L8391, '14', viewed at the Ismailia OTU, 1942.**/*V. Cashmore*

'Of course, all the different nationalities helped to add colour and character to our scene – we had Australians, Canadians, New Zealanders, Rhodesians, South Africans with us for most of the time. It is difficult to recall any instance of ill-feeling of any sort in spite of the wide differences in background, place of origin, or degree of experience of the individuals. The feeling between the various squadrons was similar. Naturally, there was rivalry, but always of a healthy, friendly variety. The only ones who did seem to have a noticeably different temperament were the Free French, when their "Lorraine" squadron of Blenheims, and three other Blenheim squadrons besides us were at Gambut early in 1942. Possibly they had not had the opportunity to practise formation flying much, but the fact remained that they were unable to keep in sufficiently close to each other when flying in tight formation was necessary. It was unfortunate therefore that whenever they took part in our multiple squadron sorties, the "Lorraine" squadron had to fly at the rear. As each squadron was stepped down from the front, this meant that the Free French were flying at the lowest height, making them the most vulnerable to ack-ack attack. Furthermore, as a result of their loose formation they were automatically more vulnerable to fighter attack under any circumstances. Having to fly at the rear not unnaturally caused them to bear a certain amount of resentment, but there was no alternative, otherwise they would endanger the aircraft behind them, as well as reducing the concentrated fire-power of the whole formation in the event of fighter attacks. Every effort was made to assist them in learning the art of close formation flying, but possibly it was the language difficulty which contributed largely to there not appearing to be the same feeling with the Free French as with other units.

'Others who played a part in keeping up the morale generally were undoubtedly the press officers. They were always welcome guests and apart from their co-operative and pleasant attitude, were frequently able to acquire things otherwise impossible to obtain. One, Fg Off Bill Tovey, who had worked on the *Daily Express* before the war, was a particularly jovial and likeable character. He was always extremely keen to go on operational trips and in spite of his large frame which took up rather more space than was comfortable in a Blenheim, he was never refused a trip when possible. Around Christmas 1941 at Gambut, he cheered us all up considerable by returning one day from a solo sortie in his wagon with a stock of Chianti – we never did find out how or from where he obtained it!

'Many people imagine that the war in the

desert took place in conditions always hot and dry, with an occasional sandstorm to add to the discomfort. Although such was mainly the case, the nights were often very cold indeed, while at times the rains could be extremely heavy causing considerable flooding in some areas. The effects of these downpours was to give an air of desolation to the already rather drab scenery. More important, they brought many problems by filling up with rain the slit trenches and the interiors of tents. Most tents were erected over specially dug hollows to give protection when the occupants had insufficient time to reach a slit trench in the event of a sudden enemy air attack on the landing ground. 14 Squadron experienced these conditions whilst at Gambut in early January 1942.

'Whilst a squadron was serving in the desert there would sometimes arise the odd occasion when it was necessary for someone to report to HQ Middle East on a matter of official business. As this meant a trip to Cairo, it was an extremely popular duty. It usually took a Blenheim about two hours for such a trip, and we would take off as early as possible, hoping to land at Heliopolis by about 8am. The programme to be aimed at was more or less of a routine pattern – we always had to be back on the squadron within two days – with, of course, whoever had to report to HQ missing out. The general idea was to go straight down to Cairo and book in at the Continental Hotel – Shepheards was considered a bit stodgy – then have a decent haircut in their saloon, a very welcome hot bath and general clean-up, proceed to Groppi's for coffee, ice cream etc. Next, drinks and lunch at Tommy's Bar, and in the afternoon either to the Heliopolis Sporting Club or the Gezira Club for a swim and afternoon tea. Back to the Continental for more drinks and dinner, followed possibly by a visit to the cinema about 9pm, after which perhaps finish up with a drink and snack at the National Hotel – eggs and bacon were usually available there around midnight. Then back to the Continental for a sleep until it was time to get up and prepare for the journey back to base. Although sometimes these trips had to be confined to within one day, it was nevertheless still possible to have an enjoyable break, and on return to imagine that one had been away for a much longer time, so refreshed did one feel.'

Geoffrey Whittard later retrained as a pilot and went on to general reconnaissance duties, ending the war in command of a Wellington squadron in Aden, flying anti-submarine patrols over the Red Sea.

Left: **Successive views of a ground-strafe of enemy transport convoy on the coastal road on 26 October 1941, seen from the nose of Blenheim IV, Z5867 of 113 Squadron RAF, piloted by Vic Cashmore.**/*V. Cashmore*

Below: **Big punch. 113 Squadron Blenheim IV with local fitment of a 20mm cannon in its nose for ground-strafing sorties; one of several squadron aircraft thus modified in 1941-42.**/*V. Cashmore*

Hurricane pilot

The entry of Italy into the war gave sharp emphasis to the Middle East RAF's need not only for greater numerical strength with which to fulfil its wide and varied responsibilities, but an overt lack of truly modern aircraft for operational effectiveness. This was especially evident among its few fighter squadrons, most of which relied on the obsolescent Gloster Gladiator biplane for 'sharp end' offensive or defensive strength. In Britain, in mid-1940, the Battle of Britain was reaching its peak of intensity, with a consequent vital need to retain all available Spitfires and Hurricanes for the UK defenders. Nevertheless, a handful of Hurricanes were slowly transferred to the Middle East, and the first squadron to receive examples was 274, formed at Amriya in August 1940 initially with Gladiators. By the end of that month 274 began to receive its first Hurricanes, and in September began operations with a mixture of both fighter types. In November the Gladiators were withdrawn and 274 became the first fully-equipped Hurricane unit in the Middle East, and played a major part in the first Libyan campaign. It again became deeply committed operationally during the 'Crusader' offensive of late 1941, and at this time was joined by a fresh pilot, Fg Off (later, Sqn Ldr) B. H. A. Playford:

'I arrived in the Western Desert at Advanced Air HQ, then at Tmini, on 24 December 1941. This was the worst Christmas Eve I have ever spent, notable only for the fact that I met Basil Embry, surely one of the bravest men ever. Next day I was awoken in my little tent around dawn by a tremendous outbreak of machine gun fire. I leapt out of bed, put on my tin hat, drew my revolver, and shot out into a slit trench. I then felt very stupid and aggrieved – it was only the ground gunners welcoming Christmas morning. A miserable Christmas – nothing but bully beef and biscuits.

Below: **Hurricane II, HL676, in factory-fresh camouflage markings, 1942, in the Middle East zone.**

'On 29 December I went to El Adem, picked up a Hurricane IIa, and met George Keefer, then a Pilot Officer, who led me to 274 Squadron at Msus. The CO was 'Sid' Linnard (until March 1942), and subsequently Sqn Ldr E. 'Dixie' Dean. We were lucky to have such experienced COs. The Flight commanders at that time were Flt Lts Andy Smith, a Canadian, and Aldridge. Andy Smith was a fantastic character. He had done something like 70 daylight shipping strikes on Blenheim Is, thoroughly deserving but never getting a gong. We had a very bad day on 26 January 1942. We went out ground-strafing all day in sections of four on the advancing Germans between Antelat and Msus. Aldridge would not fly as he said the weather was too bad, and when it was our turn my aircraft was u/s (unserviceable) but flyable. Andy Smith promised me that if I went down he would land and pick me up. I took over B Flight from Aldridge, but poor Andy was killed on 12 February.

'Morale in 274 Squadron was not particularly high at this time, but nor was it low. It was a sort of resignation. Everybody was disenchanted with the desert Hurricane. A marvellous aeroplane, built like a tank, very

Above: **Sqn Ldr Sidney Linnard DFC, seen here in the cockpit of his 80 Squadron RAF Gladiator in 1940.**

Left: **Flt Lt (later, Sqn Ldr) B. H. A. Playford, author of this chapter.**/B. H. A. Playford

Right: **The Canadian 'Wally' Conrad, later Wg Cdr DSO, DFC.**/*B. H. A. Playford*

Below right: **Sqn Ldr E. H. 'Dixie' Dean, March 1942.** / *B. H. A. Playford*

Bottom right: **Plt Off (later, Wg Cdr, DSO, DFC) George Keefer, another of the squadron's Canadian pilots.** / *B. H. A. Playford*

manoeuvrable, but hopelessly slow. The Messerschmitt Bf109F, apart from having superb armament, was nearly 100 mph faster, and climbed around 2000 feet per minute faster as well. It flew with its hood closed, whereas the hooped Hurricane hood obscured vision, so we always flew with it open. On 15 August 1942, when I had become maintenance test pilot at 243 Wing base after being wounded, I did a proper speed test in level flight in a Hurricane IIc, and at 18,000 feet I achieved a maximum speed of 200mph indicated, computed to be 270mph true! The next day I did the same on a Spitfire Vb, and at 20,000 feet obtained 240mph indicated, 320mph true. The Bf109F was faster in all respects than the desert Spitfire V. When Wally Conrad left 274 Squadron and went onto Spits, he said they were better but still not good enough. We also had a hopeless radio, the old TR9 sets, which were antiques and completely useless for air-to-air. As we had no radar, we did standby, which meant sitting in the aircraft ready for take-off for two hours at a time. As it was quite hot, even in January, after about one hour there was a great tendency to fall asleep; whereupon any evil-minded character who witnessed this would suddenly slam his transmitter on and shout down his mike, causing the sleeper to break wind violently in sheer terror!

'The food was awful but healthy. It was completely built around bully beef, hard biscuits, and a totally uneatable sausage immortalised by the name of pork and soya links. Meals consisted of a variety of bully and biscuit pie, bully and biscuit crumble, bully stew, biscuit and jam crumble, bully fritters, sausage and biscuit hash, etc. As well as this, all the water in the Tobruk area was salt, and a memorable meal could be bully fritters with mixed tinned veg, in a succulent salt water gravy, washed down with a mug of "Tobruk '42" – salt tea!

'Our two outstanding pilots were George Keefer and Wally Conrad, both Canadians. They both survived the war and, happily, are still good friends. Although our average age, I suppose, was about 22, we had two pilots, Plt Off Sammy Samuels and "Chiefy" (Flight Sergeant) O'Neill, a Canadian, who both looked incredibly young, particularly Sammy. English ladies on the tram from the junior officers' club into Alexandria often became visibly upset because Sammy looked so young. We also had an incredible cook in Ernst Honig. He came from Europe, somewhere, and *hated* Germans. If a German aircraft came into our circuit, he would rush out and start shooting at it with whatever was available. Our Intelligence NCO, Corporal Parsons, was a man of dignified bearing and highly cultured speech. He had acquired from somewhere a single springbed, which by hook or by crook he got on to the squadron transport whenever we were on the move. When in Alex he always appeared as a flight lieutenant – he believed in keeping to the highest standards of clubs and restaurants! Two of our excellent Australian NCO pilots, "Nooge" Walsh and Bill Perse, got themselves decked out as flying officers so that we could keep together when on leave. I never discovered why they weren't officers – unfortunately poor old Bill got the chop later.

'The two funniest things I recall in 274 both involved the COs of the time, Sid Linnard and Dixie Dean. We had an Australian pilot, Sgt Wildy, who had found an air raid warning siren from somewhere and spent many hours dismantling, cleaning, and oiling it and then putting it together again. Virtually as he finished it, a German bomber shot out of low cloud to drop the odd bomb, and Wildy realised that this was the perfect opportunity to sound his alarm. Everybody had already dived down the slit trenches, except – of course – the CO, Sid Linnard who, setting an

Left: **274 Squadron prepares to leave Mechili LG.**/*B. H. A. Playford*

Below: **The false 'scramble' after the 'Dixie' Dean incident (see text).**/*B. H. A. Playford*

33

example to us faint-hearted, was strolling in a dignified way from the Orderly Room tent to his own tent, completely in the open. Old Wildy cranked up his siren and this ghastly crescendo sounded like a complete Stuka squadron diving. Sid, having nowhere to go, spun round and round on the spot like a dog chasing its tail, and then collapsed into a "womb" position, with his hands clasped over his head. He was rather put out by his insubordinate pilots rolling all over the place helpless with laughter – and he wasn't too pleased with Wildy either!

'The second episode involved Dixie Dean and the aircrew loo. Our loo was a latrine bucket, surrounded by empty oil drums filled with sand. When seated, one's head and shoulders were above the level of the oil drums – and airmen had been known to salute when they passed seated officers. We usually came to "Readiness" immediately after breakfast, so there was always an undignified scramble to get to the loo as quickly as possible. The commanding officer, of course, was above all this, and would probably stroll over for a much-needed session. He had to remove his Mae West, battledress jacket, revolver, and unbutton his braces. On this particular morning he had done all this and had just got comfortably settled when I shouted "SCRAMBLE!" at the top of my voice. George Keefer started the lorry, we all jumped on, whilst Dixie *leapt* off the loo, trying to get organised in reverse order. Keefer went past him doing around 18mph and Dixie took a flying leap onto the back of the lorry, holding up his trousers with his left hand. It's strange how even the nicest people have periods when their sense of humour seems to desert them . . .

'Summing up, I suppose we were just about an average squadron. Particularly in the desert, I think the type of commanding officer made a tremendous difference. We were fortunate in our two, although I understand 274 had not always been so happily placed in the past. We definitely had a "First" and "Second XI", and – looking back with hindsight – I can see now that there were many things that I should have done as a flight commander, particularly in regard to training and organising my flight, which I failed to do.'

One Man's war

'The Middle East – Arabian nights, belly dancers gyrating to sensuous oriental music in restaurants redolent of romance and intrigue – a common association of ideas which bear little or no relevance to the hard facts of life in the Desert Air Force in the second world war. Certainly, precious few of such pleasures come to mind when recalling my own three and a half years with that remarkable collection of units and individuals from many countries. Looking back over almost two score years, the memories return mainly as a series of cameos depicting the highlights, but omitting the long spells of boredom spent contemplating the vast barren areas of sand and rock which constitute so much of the region, the heat in the day and cold of the night, the insects, and the many privations.

'It all began for me in the middle of 1941

with volunteering for overseas service while flying as a navigator/bomb aimer with 82 Squadron in Bomber Command's 2 Group on Blenheims. The actual posting when it arrived was probably the means of saving my life, because we were at Manston at that time, on attachment to 21 Squadron doing our stint of cross-Channel dashes on anti-shipping sweeps off the French and Belgian coasts. The chop rate was high, and life expectancy decidedly short! So it was without reluctance that I, together with my pilot and wireless operator/air gunner, packed kit and set off for Watton, Norfolk to collect a brand-new Blenheim IV, Z9614, just delivered from the Rootes shadow factory, and looking somewhat odd in its hybrid colour scheme of dark earth and dark green camouflage, with deep azure blue undersurfaces in place of the familiar

Below: **Baltimores of 223 Squadron RAF over Italy, December 1943. Nearest is Baltimore IV, FA591, 'H'.**

Above: **Fred Henderson, author of this chapter, with 55 Squadron RAF at Fuka, late 1941.**/*F. J. Henderson*

"sky". Equipment check and a flight test, a visit to stores for tropical kit – not forgetting the sola topee – and a series of jabs at the medical centre, a few hours' leave – back by midnight the following day.

'The first stage of our journey to Egypt was almost a routine cross-country flight to Portreath, perched high on a Cornish cliff, well positioned to receive the Atlantic weather, and there we spent a night under canvas after briefing for the next stage – to Gibraltar – with an 0800 take-off on 3 August 1941. Looking back, it seems remarkable that we relatively inexperienced air crews should accept with equanimity the notion of flying thousands of miles over a strange, and for the most part hostile, route; but when one is 20 years old the sense of adventure can be stronger than thoughts of danger. The briefing officer when handing out route maps and charts warned us to keep down near the sea when in the vicinity of Brest, to avoid detection by marauding Junkers Ju88s, for which an over-loaded Blenheim was no match. Also to be sure to adopt the correct procedure when approaching Gibraltar – the Spaniards at La Linea were not averse to loosing off a few rounds! For the ferry trip our Blenheim was provided with an extra 50-gallon fuel tank fitted in the bomb bay; this gave sufficient range to reach Gibraltar, provided that no enemy action was encountered and that the navigator kept very close to his intended track. I can still remember the aching arms I got

from pumping petrol from the bomb bay into the main tanks by means of more than a thousand strokes of a small hand pump mounted beside the pilot's seat . . .

'The take-off was uneventful, despite the heavy load of fuel, spares and kit in the well behind the wing spar, and the dim outlines of the Isles of Scilly soon appeared below us – our next tiny spot of friendly land was to be Gibraltar. After the long haul across the Bay of Biscay came the gloomy, forbidding, but very welcome sight of Cape Finisterre, spot-on track, and we then started our southward leg down the west coast of the Iberian Peninsula. By the time we were abreast of the Tagus estuary the sun was shining and our spirits soaring; around Cape St Vincent, across the Gulf of Cadiz, to be rewarded by the magnificent spectacle of the Rock of Gibraltar as we approached between the converging coasts of Europe and Africa. Putting down on the racecourse landing strip was no picnic, but we were glad to be there and to spend an evening in the town finding things in the shops, like large slabs of milk chocolate, which we had not seen for years. A magneto drop on one of the engines meant a whole day in Gibraltar and then, after a hairy take-off, we made for Malta. The distant coast of Algeria, then Vichy-controlled and decidedly unfriendly, seemed endless but we saw no other aircraft as we aimed for the little island which was the only refuge within our range. After rounding Cape Bon, Tunisia, we followed instructions by flying at a couple of hundred feet or so above the sea to avoid interception by Italian fighters from the islands of Pantelleria and Lampedusa. We saw the islands clearly enough in the sunshine but, presumably, they missed us and our approach to Malta, from the south, went smoothly enough as did our landing at Luqa. Then things changed – dispersed aircraft, shelters, bombs falling; we were on an island under siege, all rather too reminiscent of home!

'We had been warned by friendly advisers not to part with our precious Blenheim at Malta – "They'll try to persuade you to leave it there and tell you that a Sunderland is due any day which will take you on to Egypt; don't be persuaded for you could be there for months." It appeared that some air crews even had to finish their journey to the Middle East by destroyer. Well, that fate was certainly not for us – destroyers are fine for matelots, but give us an aeroplane any time, even an overloaded Blenheim. So, we resisted the blandishments of the de-briefing officer who reluctantly cleared us out of the pock-marked airfield the following morning, to spend five hours over the – sometimes – blue Mediterranean until reaching Mersa Matruh, our first call in Egypt, with the beleaguered port of Tobruk as an emergency diversion, perish the thought!

Above: **Waves of sand as a Baltimore churns up the airstrip on take-off.**/*IWM*

At Mersa Matruh we had our first experience of the desert, which was to be our home for most of the year ahead, but our stay this time was brief, because we refuelled and departed for the Maintenance Unit (MU) at Abu Sueir, near Ismailia in the Nile delta. The aircraft which we had managed to deliver intact over a journey of some 3,500 miles was dispersed, and just as well because as if to mark our arrival the Germans launched a massive air raid that very night against the MU's airfield; wiping out not only the best part of the officers' mess but also a hangar containing virtually all the available spare parts for the American aircraft, principally Tomahawks and Marylands at that time, which equipped a number of RAF and SAAF units in the area.

'However, we survived the assault and soon got our posting; to 55 Squadron, one of the Middle East's veteran units, at that time reforming at Aqir, not far from Tel Aviv in what was then called Palestine. We collected another Blenheim, an older one, V6295, and flew across the arid Sinai desert to join our

37

new unit. Tel Aviv was a revelation, a city of plenty to our eyes, and we had the opportunity of a few days' leave with visits to the Holy Places in Jerusalem and Bethlehem, and even a spell in Amman after a nightmare journey through the mountains in a rickety bus driven by a frenetic Jordanian. Then came the really serious business when the squadron was posted to Fuka, a landing ground between the railway and the road, well into the Egyptian desert but quite close to the coast, and a prominent headland for which we were to be very thankful on many occasions when returning to base in poor visibility. This was in the period when the enemy had repulsed the Wavell push, leaving Tobruk as a besieged garrison, and the front line established somewhere around Sidi Barrani, near the Libyan frontier. 55 Squadron was moved into the desert to take part in the Auchinleck push, an offensive which had an initially spectacular success driving the enemy back through most of Libya, but leaving intact too much of the now-established Afrika Korps with its Luftwaffe support.

'Our operations consisted mainly of bombing barely distinguishable targets, ammunition or petrol dumps, tanks, transport or gun positions, represented by map references in the sameness of the desert vastness. We had occasional encounters with enemy fighters and almost nightly would sojourn in slit trenches while Ju88s plastered the sparsely defended landing ground. Mostly these inflicted little damage, but there was one unforgettable night at Fuka, in November 1941, which stands out above all others as a

Above: **Baltimore crew of 223 Squadron RAF at Cazone, Foggia, Italy, late 1943. From left: Sqn Ldr Ron Clarke, the B Flt commander; Fg Off Fred Henderson; Fg Off Chapman (AG); and Fg Off Alf Brown (W/Op).**/*F. J. Henderson*

Right: **Baltimore over Italian coastal waters, 1943.**

Above: **Haven. 'Hurricane House' – the aircrew rest centre in Sharia Soliman Pasha, Cairo, during 1941-42.**/*F. J. Henderson*

nightmare of explosion and fire, when a lucky bomb at the end of a stick hit an ammunition train at the nearby depot, which was standing beside a petrol train, which in turn was alongside the fuel dump – the lot went up with spectacular results. The din was incredible and whole railway wagons were being flung into the air, parts of them landing near to our slit trench on the *opposite* side of the landing ground. The pandemonium continued for several hours, yet with the cold grey light of dawn it was found that casualties were, almost miraculously, just two badly shocked but physically unharmed fuel dump attendants who had spent the whole time in a slit trench right in the middle of the holocaust. Damage to our aircraft, dispersed around the landing ground, was not too serious and we were soon moving up behind the advancing army.

'We went first to El Gubbi, south of Tobruk, and then to another ex-Luftwaffe landing ground at Sidi bu Amud where we found a massive dugout which had been used as a Mess, and which we adopted in preference to our own tented accommodation; our only shelter apart from slit trenches and dugouts during the whole of our stay in the desert.

Conditions were never comfortable; sand, sand everywhere, many kinds of unpleasant insects, and kangaroo rats which delighted in hopping around on the corrugated roofs of the dugouts made for protection from the frequent visits of enemy night bombers. Penetrating every nook and cranny of the aircraft, the sand was a continual hazard to the ground crews, who performed wonders in keeping most of them serviceable in the appalling conditions which generally prevailed. Life was hard, food was poor, water scarce and very precious, and even sleep was often a luxury – yet morale was always good and received an occasional boost when, one day, a NAAFI van appeared, like a mirage, along the desert road. Or the time we dug up a cache of tins of evaporated milk which had been buried by retreating Germans. Conversely, we made camp one evening in poor visibility near a partially demolished building, only to discover next morning that we were among a group of hastily-dug shallow graves, and the building had been used as a mortuary!

'At one period 55 Squadron was turned into a sort of coastal unit, for which purpose the aircraft had to be flown to the MU at

Heliopolis to be repainted in two shades of blue over their desert camouflage, while retaining their azure blue undersides. These visits to Heliopolis, together with the occasional need for a major overhaul, allowed brief periods of leave in Cairo, then a city seemingly well removed from the war and, ostensibly at least, "neutral" although well patronised by Allied servicemen. The sheer luxury of a few days at the aircrew rest centre in Sharia Soliman Pasha – actually a former mansion and known colloquially as "Hurricane House" – was a marvellous chance to relax, and even afforded opportunities for socialising with the British community and visits to the opera, cinemas, and the many other delights which the fabulous Egyptian capital could, and no doubt still can, offer. The Egyptian Museum had been closed for the

duration, its treasures safely stored away, but the Gizeh Pyramids, the Sphinx, and other marvels of antiquity were all there to see. Returning to the desert after a visit to Cairo or Alexandria was a depressing anti-climax, but the good life was soon left behind when we caught up with the war.

'Anti-shipping patrols over the Mediterranean were singularly unproductive in a Blenheim because the only shipping worth attacking was out of our range, nearer to Malta, and we had many a frustrating trip, sometimes enlivened by encounters with Bf110 long-range fighters operating from Crete. Our .303in machine guns were no match for the 20mm cannons of the Bf110, but we developed a defensive technique which served us well on such occasions. We got down as close as we dared to the sea and then went around in tight circles, making it virtually impossible for the enemy to get a bead on us. The 110s usually patrolled in pairs, one maintaining top cover while the other made diving attacks, its nose spouting fire; a disconcerting sight but never, in our case, lethal for the shells would be splashing harmlessly in the sea as we turned more sharply than could the attacker, and were able to loose off our turret guns as he went past. On one occasion we saw smoke issuing from one of the engines of a Bf110, but he probably made it back to Crete.

'The over-sea losses which we did suffer were mostly attributable to engine failures more than to enemy action, because the Blenheim under desert conditions could not maintain height on one engine, and a failure near the surface would mean almost an immediate ditching in a very lonely sea. Our foray into erstwhile enemy territory was destined to be limited in duration because the reinforced Axis forces soon drove our tanks and troops back, even Tobruk falling this time, and 55 Squadron, retreating with the rest, minus most of our kit, was soon to find itself licking its wounds on a landing ground near to the Cairo – Alexandria road. The faithful Blenheims were now to be retired in favour of the much faster and better defended Martin Baltimore, virtually all production of which went to the Desert Air Force. The Baltimore, with the closely comparable Douglas Boston, was to be a mainstay of the light bomber force of the DAF for most of the remaining war years, commencing with the third and final assault on the Afrika Korps under the inspired leadership of General Montgomery.

'This personal narrative must now divert from the sands of Egypt to the lusher terrain of East Africa, because the end of an operational tour meant my transfer to 70 OTU at Kakuru, Kenya as an instructor on conversion courses from Blenheims to Baltimores; a far-flung outpost of the Desert Air Force but a vital part of that organisation; forming in effect a staging post for air crews trained in the Union of South Africa and in Rhodesia who would, in the main, be destined to join operational units in the Mediterranean zone. When, after the advance of the Allied forces through North Africa, Egypt was considered to be once again a viable location for non-operational units, 70 OTU was moved, almost literally lock, stock and barrel, thousands of miles from Nakuru to Shandur, near the banks of the Suez Canal. Our departure from East Africa was charged with mixed feelings, a genuine affection for the country after a year's stay, and excitement that the move to Egypt was bound eventually to take most of us back where the action was to be found. Moving a complete RAF unit over such a long distance was no easy task, and the motley collection of aeroplanes – Baltimores, Blenheims, Ansons, some 80 aircraft in all – had each to make the journey under their own steam. The varying speeds and ranges of the three types created many problems in staging but we got them all eventually to Shandur and business continued at the new location.

'By the time I received my posting back to operations, with a new crew, in October 1943, a foothold had been established by the Allies in southern Italy, and I was deposited after a far from comfortable ride in a Dakota, first at Catania, Sicily and then at Brindisi on the heel of Italy, where I joined 223 Squadron RAF, part of 3 SAAF Wing. Our stay at Brindisi was brief for it was soon to be too far away from

the front line being established north of Naples and south of Pescara. Moving up the Adriatic coast to the open expanse of the Foggia plain, we made our next base at Celone airfield, where we were soon in the midst of a rapidly assembling armada of aircraft of the Allied forces; British, Commonwealth, and in large numbers, the USAAF with whom we had to contend for airspace as well as parking space on the airfield. At one time we were sharing with more than 80 P-47s which flew escort to the B-17s and B-24s on nearby airfields, so closely packed that in some cases the circuits almost interlocked.

'Operations in Italy were totally different from those we had experienced in the desert. We were now in a position of air superiority and, with the Baltimore Mk IV's greater speed and vastly better defensive armament when compared with the Blenheim, plus usually a top cover of Spitfires with others in close support; we had little to fear from the Luftwaffe. The Regia Aeronautica was now, in part at least, on our side and even flew as escorts on occasion in their Macchi 202s and 205s. This by no means meant that ops in Italy were not dangerous. Our major enemy was German flak, so deadly accurate with their predicted 88mm guns that we reckoned the longest time we dare fly straight and level was about ten seconds. Our targets were many and varied – railway yards, road junctions, harbour installations, gun positions, troop concentrations, bridges; you name it, we bombed it and were effective although we suffered casualties. After the flat monotonous desert, we were now operating over the mighty Appenines, almost 10,000 feet high in places, and the winter of 1943-44 was a very hard one in Italy, with snow everywhere and the terrain hardly conducive to survival if a forced landing was necessary. We operated over enemy territory whenever the weather permitted, and froze on the ground between flights; efforts to heat our tents with petrol stoves fashioned out of oil drums led to near-disaster on a number of occasions.

'The Baltimore was able to take a great deal of punishment and frequently had to do just that as the merciless flak took its toll. In a total of 67 operations in the zone, my whole crew of four were fortunate to avoid any injuries, but damage to the aircraft was frequent; the holes being promptly patched by the stoic and calmly efficient ground crew who would sometimes work all night in the freezing open to get a damaged aircraft back on the line for the morning. We always operated in formation and rare indeed was the occasion when 223 failed to put up its full quota of 12 aircraft. My memories of those operations, carried out usually at around 12,000 feet, appear mostly as a melee of aircraft in close formation surrounded by ever-increasing numbers of dirty black, occasionally red, puffs of smoke as the flak shells burst, often so close as to rock the aircraft with the force of the blast, and at times we felt the thud as shell fragments hit the machine – only inches from my head a couple of times! The navigator/bomb aimer in a Baltimore had a wonderful view through the large transparent nose but felt rather vulnerable when under attack, and I always made a point of *sitting* on a spare steel helmet when over a target . . .

'Certain actions stand out, such as the maelstrom of aircraft and flak over the monastery at Cassino, the dawn attack on Anzio on 23 May 1944 against German gun positions as the Allied forces prepared to break out of the beach-head, and a disastrous raid near Chieti when the leading aircraft in the formation received a direct hit in its bomb bay just as it started its run onto target – the sky was filled with flaming lumps of aircraft, a complete engine whipping past our starboard wing-tip and striking the machine next to us, setting it on fire; while the aircraft abreast of the one that exploded had almost the full length of its fuselage dented in by the blast. Almost miraculously, all except the machine which had been hit returned to base, albeit some of them in very sorry states and with casualties aboard.

'As the spring and summer of 1944 progressed, and the better weather at least removed some of the natural hazards of flying, operations continued along similar lines but now included some diversions to Yugoslavia to co-operate with Tito's partisans. An extraordinary feature of these raids was that after crossing the Adriatic Sea we would rendezvous with Spitfires which were operating from the small island of Vis, within sight of the enemy-occupied Dalmatian coast! Our base had, with the advance of the ground forces, moved first to Termoli (Biferno), then to Pescara. A further move to Ancona was imminent but the days of 223 Squadron were numbered. RAF personnel were being dispersed as the unit re-equipped with Martin Marauders and renumbered as 30 SAAF Squadron, thereby making 3 SAAF Wing an all-South African formation. Thus my long spell with the Desert Air Force ended when I boarded a 24 Squadron Dakota at Naples for the journey home to the United Kingdom – arriving at Hendon almost in formation with a flying bomb. The war was obviously still with me – but the desert seemed a long way off . . .'

Below: **Marauders of 3 Wing SAAF on PSP dispersal strips preparing for a sortie, 1944./***IWM*

Iron Maidens

The history of the RAF's Armoured Car companies goes back – officially – to December 1921 – when No 1 Armoured Car Company RAF, was formed at Heliopolis for support of RAF air operations in Iraq; followed in August 1922 by the formation of No 2 AC Coy for work in the Transjordan zone of operations. By 1925 the RAF's 'Iron Maidens' reached their peak strength, with a total of five separate AC Companies – all based in the Middle East. Their largely unheralded contributions to the RAF's efforts prior to 1939 were prodigious, and when war came to

North Africa from 1940, the armoured car crews became the RAF's equivalent of the Army's Long Range Desert Group and SAS, in certain respects. Crews operated almost independently, often well out of re-supply range for long spells, and leading a roving 'pirate' life; a virtual private army in outlook and individualism. Their roles throughout the various North African campaigns were myriad – airfield defence (their motto, 'First in – Last out'), forward reconnaissance, recovery of abandoned tanks on occasion, 'ghost' strike formations which appeared like phantoms from the desert, struck hard, and vanished again like will o' the wisps. Yet another role was rapid identification and location of suitable stretches of bald desert for use as RAF advanced landing grounds as the highly fluid ground battles swayed east and west.

At the outbreak of war No 1 AC Company was based at Habbaniyah, Iraq and when that RAF station was besieged by the hostile forces of Raschid Ali in May 1941, the armoured cars' crews played a vital role both in defence and offence against the attacking Iraqi forces. Later that year the company began a 3,000-mile drive to Egypt, and one driver was Eric Cant, now manager (appropriately, perhaps . . .) of a large garage in Beverley, Yorkshire:

'On arrival in Egypt we formed up at Helwan, where we were attached to the 7th Armoured Division and moved straight up into the desert

*Above: HMAC Explorer of **No 1 Armoured Car Company, RAF**./E. Cant*

Right: **Eric Cant (left) and 'Iron Maiden' crew of No 1 AC Company**./E. Cant

for the "Crusader" offensive. The 7th Armoured – the original "Desert Rats" – were a really tough mob, and a credit to the Army. Mainly regulars, they had come from India where terrain or type of fighting was very different. It was a real experience seeing those "hard nuts" going into action – they really got stuck in.

'Our job was to follow close behind and to the fringes of the advance – or just ahead of the retreat, as the case might be – to find suitable sites for use as landing grounds. These might be areas of firm, level ground of the right size, or existing abandoned strips which had not been too badly damaged or demolished. On finding a suitable site, we would survey it, pace out the required distances, assess the amount of work needed to clear stones and scrub, fill holes or soft spots,

etc; then radio this information back. Work parties were never far behind us, and they would be diverted to the location. As soon as we handed over to them, we moved on to look for the next site. If it was an existing strip, then we would give a general opinion as to how long it would take to get it serviceable, clear booby traps, wrecks etc. If it had been too badly hacked about, we'd look around the edges to see if a new strip could be laid alongside, as conditions generally would usually be favourable for a strip in the immediate vicinity. These strips didn't have to be anything terrific – just enough for the fighters to land and take off from, and for transport aircraft to fly in supplies.

'When we first went up into the desert we were still using our old Rolls-Royces. We were trained to a very high level on these and thus operated efficiently, but they had their problems. Basically very reliable vehicles, they had been *over*-maintained during the period prior to the Raschid Ali rebellion; in a word, we had "bulled" them far too much. Every pipe and nut had been polished constantly to perfection, but in the event some had been polished almost through and were consequently weakened. Constant training in rapid wheel changes and engine stripping had worn the threads on nuts and bolts etc. As a result in war conditions we suffered some unserviceability due to failure of these parts.

'The single Vickers .303in machine gun was no real armament, and we had no great confidence in our ability to defend ourselves, or to do any real damage to the enemy if we were forced into a fight. However, morale was generally very good and although we usually had little idea of what was going on, we worked well as a set of good teams. Everything happened so fast in the desert; there was little time during offensives to find out what was happening – it was just a case of into the cars and go!

'We went out in groups of three or four cars, plus a wireless van and breakdown

Left: **'Butch, MC', an RAF armoured car company's canine mascot until his death in action in Libya.**

Below: **No 1 AC Company prepared to set off into the desert.**/*E. Cant*

vehicle, and were fully self-sufficient. Each car carried its own food, water and fuel, and each crew cooked for themselves. We slept by or under the cars – just sleeping rough. There was usually no time to make bivouacs or whatever as we would be off again at first light. General maintenance was done wherever we happened to stop, and re-supply was no great problem. Army re-supply organisations were usually five to ten miles back behind the lines, and we merely sent one of the trucks back to rendezvous and pick up whatever we needed.

'As a result of what we were doing we saw very little of the rest of the RAF – it was mainly the Army we maintained contact with – but we certainly did see quite a lot of the other side's air force! On occasion we had skirmishes with the enemy, usually when we had gone forward a bit too quickly and got ahead of our main armour. Our opponents were there with their own scouting armoured cars – but the general idea was to get out of each other's way as quickly as possible! However, it was standard practice for each side to call down air strikes on the other and we were often

attacked by Stukas – really very unpleasant indeed. When any such attack developed we spread out as widely as possible and kept going fast. When we got anti-aircraft machine guns on the turret tops our gunners certainly blazed away back, but it was hard on the nerves; I've had the man sitting next to me screaming as the bombs fell. Yet on looking back, not one car was ever hit during any such attack.

'During the static periods between offensives there was little for us to do and we took the opportunity to rest up, undertake training, maintenance and cleaning of equipment. When the Gazala offensive started in mid-1942, however, British armour losses were terrible, and we lost several Rolls-Royces, and were pulled out to re-equip with Humbers. These were much more modern, well equipped, and well armoured cars, but we were given no time to train on them. We were simply re-equipped, briefed, then virtually thrown straight back on operations; taking part in the retreat back to Alamein, during which Tobruk was lost. Initially, as the Humber was a very different vehicle, we weren't as efficient as we had been with the old Rolls-Royces, but we soon learned. We were now attached to the 17/21st Hussars – the "Cherrypickers" – who were also Humber-equipped.

'Our Rolls-Royces had all carried names from the pre-war days. I had driven *HMAC Explorer* first, then the *Avenger*. No names were carried on the Humbers, however – in the summer of 1942 the war had become a much more serious business. Each car carried a crew of three in either case; driver, gunner and commander. Once we got back behind the Alamein line our activities ceased again until the big push in November 1942. I did not take part in the latter, for on arrival in El Alamein I was sent back to Habbaniya, and from there to England for non-operational duties.'

Below: 'All-purpose' desert truck, complete with radio, tool chest, spare Jerricans of petrol, et al./*E. Cant*

Bottom: Well and truly bogged down – a common hazard in the soft-crust sections of the treacherous desert./*E. Cant*

Fighter pilot

Credited with at least 16 combat victories during a three-year spell of operations with the Desert Air Force, Canadian J. F. Edwards, 'Stocky' or 'Eddie' to his friends – commenced his desert service as a young Sergeant in January 1942, and eventually left the Middle East zone in late 1944 as a Squadron Leader, DFC & Bar, DFM. His own account of those years exemplify the experiences of many fighter pilots of the DAF during those fateful years:

'The ship stopped at Freetown, West Africa, where a number of pilots were named to proceed overland to the Cairo area. We pilots were flown via Sunderland flying boat to Takoradi, to an RAF ferry unit on the west coast of Africa. I flew the first four legs of the trip, but then my Hurricane was declared unserviceable, so I returned to Takoradi in a DC3, was check out in a Blenheim IV bomber, and then flew as second pilot across the continent, arriving at Heliopolis aircrew Pool on 29 December 1941. From here I was posted to 94 Squadron on 15 January 1942 and was transported by Bombay aircraft to join the squadron at Antelat, a western desert airfield some 180 miles south of Benghazi. As the Bombay landed near the Mess tent at Antelat, we were welcomed by two Ju88s appearing out of the clouds and dropping bombs on the airfield, accompanied by very loud ack-ack.

'The state of 94 Squadron appeared somewhat demoralised; in particular, we were told that there were only six pilots left on the squadron and few aircraft. Seven pilots, including the commanding officer and one Flight commander, had been shot down the day before by Messerschmitt Bf109s. We met two or three bedraggled pilot types in the Mess and learned that the others were on cockpit stand-by down near the airstrip, but they wouldn't be scrambled because their Hurricanes were over their wheels in mud and couldn't even be taxied. This was my introduction to an operational squadron in the western desert . . .! At this time the Army had reached the limits of its first westward advance and had run out of steam and resources. From all appearances the area was a shambles. Retreating army personnel said that the front had been broken and the Jerries were now advancing – Rommel was beginning one of his famous pushes. In the early hours of the morning following our arrival, the four remaining Hurricanes were towed to drier ground and flown away east to more friendly territory, then the squadron camp was struck and everyone departed east across the desert.

'94 Squadron was re-grouped south of Tobruk at LG 110 and converted to Kittyhawks on 1 February 1942. On 14 February the squadron brought their new

Below: **Sgt James Francis Edwards in his 94 Squadron RAF Kittyhawk, AK739, FZ-R, in February 1942. The squadron code letters FZ were later changed to GO.**/*J. F. Edwards*

Kittyhawks to Gambut to re-commence operations, led by a new CO, Sqn Ldr E. M. 'Imshi' Mason, DFC, a famous desert pilot with 17 victories credited. However, the very next day, 15 February, 94 Squadron suffered another serious setback in the air this time over the enemy airfield at Martuba. With only a few hours of conversion training on Kittyhawks, Mason led eight aircraft on a sweep and strafing mission in an attempt to catch the Bf109s on the ground at Martuba. One or two alert Messerschmitt pilots saw the raid approaching and were able to get airborne, climb up, and come down on 94 Squadron as they crossed the field. They shot down the CO and four others.* This

* All five RAF aircraft were shot down by Oberfeldwebel Otto Schulz of II Gruppe, JG 27.

unfortunate operation proved conclusively that the Kittyhawk, although some improvement over the Hurricane, was no match for the Bf109 in the hands of an experienced pilot.

'On 16 February the squadron withdrew to LG 115 for further training with Sqn Ldr MacDougall as commanding officer. Here the squadron began flying a new type of formation, the "Finger Four", with four aircraft in line-abreast. On 20 March we moved up again, this time to Gasr el Arid, to resume operations. Nevertheless, the squadron continued to lose both experienced and inexperienced pilots to Bf109s; consequently the unit was next repatriated to the Delta area on 10 May, and I was then posted to 260 Squadron. With five other pilots I walked across the airfield to join this squadron, which was also flying Kittyhawk 1s. By this time I

Right: **Wing Commander J. F. Edwards DFC, DFM.**/*Public Archives of Canada*

Below: **Domestic panorama of 260 Squadron RAF at LG 109, 1941.**/*M. Gidman*

had approximately 60 hours on the Kittyhawk, and while I felt quite comfortable with the aeroplane, I still knew very little about flying it in combat against the 109s.* In my estimation the Kittyhawk Mk 1 was not an easy aircraft to fly properly and as a result we lost a good number of pilots whilst training, and some experienced Hurricane pilots just flatly refused to fly it, preferring to go back to Hurricane squadrons.

'Regarding the Kittyhawk 1, I found that one had to have a very strong right arm to control this aircraft during most manoeuvres. For instance, while dive-bombing the aircraft would pick up speed very quickly in the dive but had a great tendency to roll to the right. One could trim this out reasonably well with the left hand, but even then when one pulled up the fighter wanted to roll to the left quite violently; so I learned to trim out about halfway in the dive and hold the control stick central by bracing my arm against my leg and the cockpit wall. This way I found that I had more control and didn't have to take off so much trim when pulling out and the speed was reduced. However, it was distracting to have one's left hand on the trim all the time when it should have been on the throttle. Perhaps from this example the instability of the aircraft in the lateral plane at changing speeds can be understood – thus in a dogfight with violent changes of speed it was all one could do simply to fly the Kittyhawk. To avoid being shot down needed a head on a swivel – to look down into the cockpit even for a split second with 109s about was sure death. Since the Kittyhawk could fishtail and skid violently if not flown smoothly, which left little chance of hitting anything, I had the mercury ball portion of a needle and bank instrument placed right below my gunsight so that I could see it all the time, even without staring at it – this took all the guesswork out of flying smoothly.

* In fact, by then Edwards had already been credited with two combat victories while with 94 Squadron.

'The Kittyhawk Mk II (P-40F) with Packard-Merlin engine – the Americans called it the Warhawk, but in 260 Squadron we called it the "Gosh-Hawk" – was a definite improvement in lateral stability over the Mk I. 260 Squadron flew Kittyhawk IIs from September 1942 to 17 December 1942, when we received Kittyhawk IIIs with many modifications and improvements by the end of the Tunisian campaign. Eventually with the Mk III, the Kittyhawk became a good stable fighting aircraft, though it never did have enough power or climbing ability compared with a 109 or Spitfire. All Kittyhawks had six .50in guns – excellent for strafing and blowing up ground targets. However, one annoying feature was the gun stoppages in the desert. When ground-strafing one could count on firing all ammunition without problems, but in dogfighting excessive "G" forces came into play – the guns nearly always packed up after a few bursts, leaving the fighter in a most perilous position. The 109s never appeared to have any problems with their nose cannons – that big gaping hole in the centre of a white spinner with black puffs of smoke emitting from it.

'The cruising speed of the Kittyhawk II was reasonably fast, and about equal to that of the Spitfire V, while that of the Mk III compared to the Spitfire IX. However, the Kittyhawk didn't jump forward in answer to the throttle being advanced to full power, nor did it climb worth a damn compared with the Spitfire. It would turn inside the 109, but not as easily as a Spitfire. When the squadron's "tame" Bf109F flew with the Kittyhawks we found it necessary to throttle back to about 72 per cent power to stay with the formation. The Bf109s definitely flew at higher cruising speeds – about 290/300mph – when operating with two or four aircraft.

'The month of June 1942 was another difficult period for everyone when the Germans were preparing for their advance, and 260 Squadron was primarily assigned to bomber escort duties over enemy concentrations. The enemy lines were only 25-30 minutes flying time from the Gambut airfields, so we would fall in as escort as the bombers passed over the field. All Kittyhawks carried 500lb of bombs which we would drop after seeing the bombers safely on their way home; on most occasions we would go down and strafe after dropping the bombs. During that June the whole battle area appeared to be engulfed in dust and haze up to 12,000 feet. The sun shone through the haze with full intensity making the canopy tops glare. Messerschmitts were always over the target areas and attacked out of the sun as we turned.

'But the end of June the squadrons were in retreat, leap-frogging back in order to provide cover for our ground forces. At that time we

Left: '**Stocky' Edwards in his 94 Squadron Kittyhawk, February 1942.**/*J. F. Edwards*

Above: **Unidentified NCO pilot of 260 Squadron RAF in Hurricane Z4266, MF-E, circa November 1941.**/*M. Gidman*

didn't know why, but the Luftwaffe made no attempt to really support their advancing army. All desert squadrons re-grouped along the Alexandria-Cairo line and stabilised for the first time. Personnel were able to get a much-needed rest and change in Alexandria for a few days. Many new pilots arrived on the squadron and intensive training took place, while bomber escorts and sweeps continued. The squadron seemed to take on new life and knit together as a fighting team. By then – mid-September 1942 – I was leading the squadron on occasions as a sergeant. Administrative paper work had a very low priority. There was no feeling that we would move further east, or give up Alex or Cairo; it was a matter of recouping, building up, and going forward again. It was a different story now that our supply lines were down to almost zero, and it was the enemy's that were stretched out for miles. Many great air battles were fought over or near the Alamein line during July-November 1942. Our squadrons seemed to take on new strength and now there were three Spitfire squadrons operating in the area, making the 109s look up for the first time. We still lost pilots to 109s and ground fire, but the Luftwaffe was being hurt as their ablest sharp-shooters began to fall to Allied fighters. After the advance began in November 1942, it wasn't long before the bomber bases were too far behind the lines, so 260 Squadron joined 239 Wing with a primary role of dive-bombing and strafing, and occasional escort duties when the bombers were able to move up. This role continued until the end of the Tunisian campaign.

'Apart from flying, life in the desert generally was good – everyone soon adapted and learned to get along with the bare essentials. There was always a high degree of camaraderie, of living and fighting together, of trying to get the most of what was necessary to fight the enemy. Everyone was too busy or

engrossed to become bored or lonely. Personally, I never thought much of being anywhere else – in fact, I was having the time of my life. Little things didn't matter – only important things counted. Uniforms and parades were unheard of and unnecessary, only rank insignia were worn with any regularity. There were no such things as social functions, parties, or gatherings that might promote anyone's rank or position. At times during trying periods there would be shortages of food, with only bully beef and hard tack to eat, and only enough water to make tea, brush one's teeth, and wash one's face, but nobody went hungry or suffered ill effects. Most times there were lots of extras supplied in tins – tinned bacon, potatoes and fruit from South Africa and Australia – so there never were really any complaints regarding messing. Besides, there was no one to complain to, or no one cared to listen to such trivia. There were times we were able to shoot gazelle for fresh meat, or even quail. Except for three or four landing grounds such as Martuba, El Adem, Gazala, all Kittyhawk squadrons operated from new LGs levelled out of the desert some 20/30 miles from the coast. As a result we were seldom bothered by flies or other crawly creatures that were most surely prevalent at the older bases along the coast. Most important, there were none of the diseases common to inhabited areas.

'It should be noted, incidentally, that there was *no* air traffic control as such at the desert landing grounds throughout the entire desert campaigns, or even into Tunisia. Remarkable, when one contemplates a situation where four squadrons, sometimes more, operated from the same LG without mishap or waiting for take-off or landing. Usually the squadrons operated together, but on one occasion they conducted separate sorties. Except for the original airfields which were built along the coast, all others were simply graded out of the

desert sand, approximately half a mile square, with a squadron widely dispersed on each side of the square. Group HQ would lay on operational duties; for example, for a bomber escort mission; Group HQ would notify the squadrons in order – close, medium, or top cover, or whatever, in relation to the bombers. The bombers formed up over their own field and then flew over the escort's field at 2/3000 feet. When the bombers were seen approaching, all engines of the escort squadrons started up. As the bombers made a wide circuit of the field, the top cover escort took off first – usually 12 aircraft almost line-abreast across the field from their dispersal area. On take-off there was no lagging because one could be completely blinded by the dust kicked up from the leading aircraft's prop-wash. This was all very well, provided the leader was lined up directly across the field to allow room for the aircraft on the extremes. There were occasions when pilots not fully aware of such hazards found themselves charging through dispersal areas, in amongst tents and slit trenches, while attempting to get airborne!

Top: **Cheerful gaggle of 260 Squadron's pilots, circa November 1941.**/*M. Gidman*

Above: **Pre-ops briefing for 260 Squadron, mid-1942. From left: Coley; Bernier; Shepherd; Cundy; Black; Fallows; Takvor; Aitchison.**/*J. F. Edwards*

'Secondly, the medium bomber cover took off across the field from their dispersal, and finally the close cover squadron would follow from their side. By the time the bomber formation had completed a wide circuit of the field, all escort squadrons were in position around and above them, and the lot set course. On return to base the squadrons landed in reverse order to take-off. There was little waiting to land – the 109s had come into the circuit occasionally and caught aircraft with their wheels down. All pilots, therefore, learned to approach the field and land in the shortest time possible. Squadrons arranged landing priorities in the air, over the R/T, when necessary, but there was *no* air traffic control from the ground.

'The remarkable ability of the RAF to leap-frog its units in retreat as well as in advance to ensure full support to the ground troops seemed at times incredible. Someone had to be there in advance to prepare fields for the aircraft arrivals, usually on completion of an operation from the previous base. As the advance proceeded into Tripolitania, entire airfields had to be levelled out of the desert because of a shortage of landing grounds in new battle areas. Advance troops, including all squadron personnel who could be spared, would often pitch in with shovels and prepare a runway. While the desert was really a healthy place to live and operate, with only minor ailments throughout the year, the ground crews suffered several privations. With no let-up from dawn to dusk, day after day, for more than two years for many, they were literally slaves to flying operations. No word good enough can be expressed to praise the ground crews' outstanding achievements

in keeping our aircraft flying throughout the desert war.

'Flying over the desert was an experience in itself. Seen from above it initially offered no evidence of habitation or life. There were shades of sand and brown with dark lines or spots intermixed, and to the novice this is best described as "Bundoo" – nothing of note for miles in the great vastness below. Some pilots had more trouble finding their way around than others because as novices they could be right over an airfield and not recognise anything at first glance. Then the sun glinting off a perspex canopy or other object on the ground would help bring a whole camp into focus, with a very obvious airstrip in the middle. Of course, there was the Mediterranean coastline running roughly east-west, which everybody could recognise and set course from some point on the coast.

'Bomber escort missions were sometimes flown out to sea, crossing back in near the target area, especially when said target was on the coast. Airfields such as El Daba, Gazala, Martuba, and enemy troop concentrations along the coast roads were attacked from out to sea. Most times operations were conducted over the desert where the coastline might be visible in the distance, depending on altitude flown. Strafing missions were flown right down on the deck, where surprise and accuracy in locating targets depended solely on the leadership of an experienced desert pilot. Experience could only be gained by actual close contact with the environment in hours flown, time in the area, and combat.

'The main and only reliable navigational aid in the desert was the sun. The desert *was* the sun, they were as one – sometimes annoying,

sometimes a hindrance, but always helpful when attacking or navigating. With experience one learned to read the desert floor by light and shadow. Every object, regardless of shape or size, cast a shadow, and by discerning these contrasts and knowing the actual ground environment in any given area, it was possible to understand and appreciate alien objects and movement amidst the normal surroundings. It was common practice to go down on the deck 60 to 80 miles from base and, with the aid of compass or directional gyro, align with the position of the sun, set course, and arrive over our own field. The sun was an important factor in all navigational and operational flying in the desert.

'In 260 Squadron we were fortunate in having Sqn Ldr O. V. Hanbury as commanding officer, who was probably one of the best all-round fighter leaders in the desert. He was a veteran of the Battle of Britain and completed two tours of ops in the desert. He was the CO when I joined 260 in May 1942, went off ops about 17 August for a rest, but returned to the squadron on 4 November 1942 and continued as CO until the end of the fighting in Tunisia. In the air he was the "steely-grey" type, intent on destroying the enemy, and he expected the same from all his pilots. There were no excuses, no short-cuts, no line-shooting allowed or displayed at any time. He commanded respect from everyone on the squadron. When the North African campaign ended in Tunisia, it seemed to come as a great anti-climax. The squadron was riding high on the crest of achievements. It had worked and flown as a highly capable fighting unit – and then it was all over. There were more than a dozen pilots who had

survived the lot from August 1942 back on the Alexandria-Cairo line. In fact, Flt Lt Bill Stewart, who joined 260 Squadron with me in May 1942 and was now a Flight commander, had seen it through unscathed. However, the biggest shock to the squadron at that time was the loss of Sqn Ldr Hanbury. As a reward, following the termination of the Tunisian campaign, the 239 Wing Leader, Wg Cdr Burton, and his four squadron commanders including Hanbury, were flown back to England for a few days leave. On the return flight their aircraft was shot down by a Ju88 over the Bay of Biscay. Sad, for there went many good leaders. And alas for the four Kittyhawk squadrons, any deserved awards or promotions would not be forthcoming. The remaining pilots were left to the dubious mercy of the HQ Cairo staff, to be dispersed wherever . . .

Top: **Erks of 260 Squadron RAF servicing a unit Hurricane at El Bassah, circa August 1941.** */M. Gidman*

Above: **Kittyhawk FL272, HS-W, of 260 Squadron at El Bassa in February 1943, with attendant Coles crane.**/*via F. F. Smith*

'In early December 1943 I was posted to 417 Squadron, RCAF in 244 Wing, RAF as supernumerary, and flew 11 sorties with them. The Wing also included 92, 145 and 601 Squadrons, RAF. We operated off a strip or single runway of PSP (Perforated or Pierced Steel Planking) that was interlocked in sections. The base was referred to as Canne, near Termoli, about 80 miles north of Foggia on the east side of Italy, on the Adriatic coast. This was a complete change from the desert – the weather was wet with mud everywhere – the normal condition for the winter season.

The countryside had green fields and trees, and high mountains in the central regions. We flew Spitfire VIIIs – all brand new and what beautiful aircraft to fly! Normal cruising speed wasn't much faster than the Kittyhawk III, but one could open the throttle and feel an immediate and positive response. The Spitfire was as fast as any 109 and could catch a 109 in a climb or dive. My experience of flying the Bf109 was that as speed increased the stick forces also increased, indicating very heavy wing loadings, whereas the Spitfire was light on elevators at all speeds. Indeed, it was fast and smooth, making it a real joy to fly. In order to fully appreciate the outstanding qualities of a Spitfire, pilots should have been first required to do a tour of ops on Kittyhawks!

'On 19 December 1943 I joined 92 "East India" Squadron as a Flight commander, and in January 1944 the squadron moved to the west side of Italy, north of Naples, to a strip called Marcinionize, to cover the Allied landings at Anzio. The squadron's daily operations were to patrol the Anzio beach-head, providing air cover and air superiority over the battle zone. No more ground-strafing or dive-bombing, just patrolling at 20,000 feet-plus, on the look-out for hostiles which were very scarce. No more incidents of being jumped by 109s – when we did meet the Luftwaffe we had to chase them to catch them. Then, on 7 March 1944, I was promoted to Squadron Leader and given

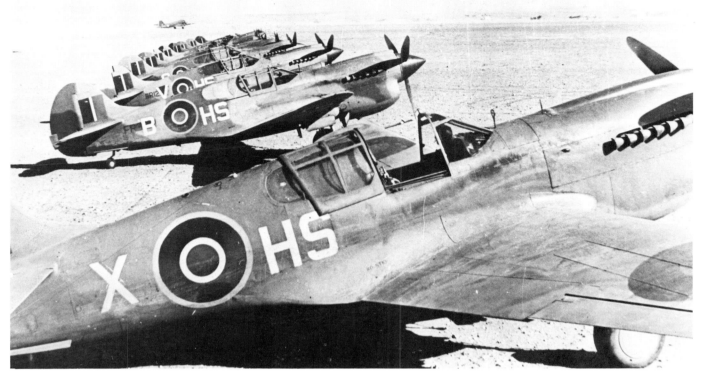

command of 274 Squadron. So it was back to Canne again on the east coast, and back to Spitfire Vs.

'Needless to say, I was very happy to take command of such a grand bunch of desert warriors. I'd flown a Spitfire V at the gunnery school at El Ballah between my two ops tours, and after 80 hours flying time felt that I knew it well. 274's Spitfires were old desert veterans as well, handed down from 244 Wing which was now flying Spitfire VIIIs. So, for operations it was a return to bomber escorts, dive-bombing, and strafing. However, I had only flown a few operations with 274 when, en route to a strafing sortie over Frosinone my aircraft developed an internal glycol leak over the mountans and I was forced to land on a mountain top. I was able to return to my squadron about seven days later, but about this time 274 Squadron was ordered back to England to bolster forces for D-Day. The whole squadron, together with 80 and 229 Squadrons, were stowed aboard a ship to the UK on 10 April 1944, and arrived in Britain on 23 April. On arrival everyone was granted seven days leave, and we then reformed at Hornchurch with Spitfire IXs. There were certainly mixed feelings about quitting operations in Italy after so long a time as a front line squadron, and most ground personnel had forgotten that anything so nice as returning home could happen to them . . .'

Above: **Line-up of 260's Kittyhawks west of Marble Arch, Tripoli in November 1942. 'X' was Sqn Ldr Hanbury's aircraft, while 'B' was Edwards' machine. In distance a Dakota trundles by.**/*J. F. Edwards*

Below: **Spitfire V, BR523 of 92 Squadron RAF on return from a sortie.**/*Australian War Memorial*

Springbok combat

A native of Transvaal, South Africa, Charles Laubscher joined the RAF prior to the war, and his first operational posting came when he joined 274 Squadron in the western desert early in 1941, just at the tail-end of Wavell's first advance. Almost immediately, he became part of a detachment sent to reinforce the air defence of Malta and was incorporated there into 261 Squadron, flying Hurricanes. Scoring several victories over Malta, Laubscher stayed with 261 when it was withdrawn to Palestine in May 1941, and in January 1942, as a flight lieutenant, he joined 2 Squadron, SAAF as commander of its A Flight. The squadron then flew Curtiss Tomahawks, and after two months rest and work-up training, it moved back to operations on 13 March:

'On 6 April 1942 the squadron flew top cover to Bostons raiding Martuba. Three aircraft in my flight were forced to return to base early, so I roved alone above the squadron. We were attacked during the homeward run by a 109F, diving almost vertically, about five miles south-east of Martuba. I turned tightly to port in the standard evasive action and saw him half-roll onto his back which enabled him to lay off a deflection. I pulled on my stick to tighten the turn and my Tomahawk promptly went into a spin. Straightening out at about 5,000 feet, I found myself in a hornet's nest of 109Fs flying in sections of three, line-astern, at different altitudes. I saw at once that one section would pass almost directly ahead of me at a range of approximately 250 yards, so I laid off a full beam deflection on their No 3 and fired a long burst. His port wing dropped and he slid into a gentle dive, but I didn't wait to see what happened to him, heading back to our own lines at full throttle.

'I was then attacked by two more 109s but out-turned them easily and put my nose down in a power dive to the south-east, levelling off at about 300 feet. North-west of Gazala I saw that a section of three 109Fs, flying in echelon port, were overhauling me, but as I now guessed that two were almost certainly pilots in training, I steep-turned to port back towards them and did a head-on attack on No 3. I fired a good burst into him as we closed without experiencing any return fire, then immediately did a steep turn to port and headed back to Gazala, ducking over the escarpment down to the level of the mud flats. Only two aircraft were now closing on me,

Below: **Scramble – Tomahawks of a SAAF squadron get airborne.**/*IWM*

more appropriately in line astern, but I had not seen what had happened to their No 3. I waited until they were committed to a quarter stern attack from the left, then turned tightly towards them at about 50 feet above the ground. They were obviously unable – or too nervous – to turn as tightly as I did at this almost zero altitude. As they overshot I again headed for our lines which were now close, and they left me. I prayed that our army types would not be trigger-happy but I was low enough for our chaps to see my roundels and no shots were fired. I thought I could only claim a probable and a damaged, but a telephone call was received from the bomber Wing stating that a rear gunner had seen an aircraft go in south-east of Martuba. As no other aircraft had fired a shot, this was clearly my 109F and I was able to claim it as destroyed.

'On 24 April I was leading a section of four Tomahawks on a sweep over the Bir Hacheim-Gazala area when we caught four 109Fs napping below us. I fired a good burst into one and he went down apparently out of control, but I never saw him go in as I turned back at the others. I didn't manage to get in another shot, but my No 2 destroyed one.

'Next day 2 Squadron was on stand-by. 4 Squadron (SAAF) had now been re-equipped with Kittyhawks and I borrowed one of these for a brief test flight. I tried out the guns and was impressed by their fire-power and the tracer was clearly visible. I was also impressed by the machine's power and manoeuvrability, the excellent field of vision from the cockpit – and not least by the pilot's relief tube! I landed after 20 minutes and was taxying in when all squadrons of the Wing were scrambled. I at once took off again without changing aircraft,

with 11 Tomahawks from 2 Sqn, 12 Kittyhawks from 4 Sqn, and 12 Kittyhawks from 260 Squadron. Climbing at full bore – the control's orders were "Buster" – all aircraft were virtually in a straight line, hoping to catch a Stuka squadron which had bombed our troops at Tobruk. The squadron at the north end of the line (No 4, I believe) tallyhoed as they saw the Stukas flying low over the Gulf of Gazala, and the other two squadrons swung north-west towards them in time to be met by a mixed gaggle of 109Fs and Macchi 202s, numbering about 35-40 aircraft. What I believe to have been the biggest dogfight of the desert war developed.

'One minute two or three of us were firing at a single enemy aircraft, and the next we were dodging attacks from two or three 109s or Macchis. A classic remark heard over the R/T came from Syd Cohen of 4 Squadron who was being give a particularly torrid time by four Bf109Fs – "Christ! Do these bloody Germans think I'm the *only* Jew in the South African Air Force? . . ." While weaving around I saw a 109F creeping up the tail of a Kittyhawk about 300 feet below and the same distance ahead of me. I yelled over the R/T, "Kittyhawk below me – TURN, for Christ's sake, TURN!" He must have heard me loud and clear for he went into a steep turn to starboard immediately, followed by the 109F which could not lay off sufficient deflection. I cut the corner diving towards them, allowed as much deflection as I dared – my reflector sight's dot was on the Kittyhawk's fuselage! – and fired a long burst. I saw good strikes on the 109's fuselage and wings and he slid slowly downwards into a steep dive. I couldn't follow him as I had to dodge an aircraft attacking me from my port stern quarter. However, I

Below left: **C. J. Laubscher with his 2 Squadron SAAF Tomahawk in the western desert, 1942.**/*C. J. Laubscher*

Below: **C. J. Laubscher in the cockpit of Tomahawk TA-L, 2 Squadron SAAF.** / *C. J. Laubscher*

attacked another 109F head-on and saw a streak of fire along his cowling as I passed over him. I then chased another 109F to Tmimi, firing at long range. Tracers appeared to strike him, but tracers can be deceptive and he didn't go down. I was then nearly jumped twice by 109s but out-manoeuvred these and chased another out to sea, but couldn't catch him so returned to the combat area. The sky was now clear of aircraft so I headed back to base, the guns almost limp from their efforts! The armourers later told me I'd fired 1,100 rounds. I claimed one 109F probably destroyed and one damaged. The Wing lost six aircraft in this engagement, but we heard later that enemy losses were thought to have been similar.

'In the weeks which followed 2 Squadron, SAAF was also re-equipped with Kittyhawks and it was a section of four of these which I was leading on a patrol over the coastal area on about 5 June when I saw four dots in line-abreast on the horizon to the west, which we soon identified as Bf109Fs. I turned the section southwards and climbed towards the sun. Unfortunately, they saw us almost simultaneously and also turned and climbed up-sun. We converged some miles inland and although we had climbed with them, more by willpower than horse-power, they had gained about 1,000 feet in height on us in the intervening period. I looked around for the other members of my section and – to my dismay – found that I was alone! I learned later that they'd been unable to hold the climb with me and two had gone into spins, while the third had to dive to avoid spinning. I levelled off when I saw the 109s splitting up. They then positioned themselves at the four points of the compass, bracketing me in the centre.

'The first attacked from five o'clock. I turned sharply up at him and he pulled up and away from me. Immediately I did a 180-degrees turn to meet the expected attack from the opposite direction and he also pulled away when he saw that I could bring my guns to bear. Then it was No 3's turn from the port quarter – then No 4's. I was sweating profusely, but felt quite confident as I realised they were looking for an easy victim and were not prepared to shoot it out. This pecking from different directions continued for about five minutes – although it seemed nearer 50 – and then they climbed slightly and began circling me. I was busy fixing their positions in my mind when I suddenly realised that there were now only three aircraft in the circle. I expected an attack from behind and almost stood my machine on its tail as I swung left and right, searching the sky above and below me, but he was nowhere to be seen. I knew that he wouldn't have left me – sitting duck if ever there was one. I was so flabbergasted that

I flew straight and level for about 30 seconds to collect my wits. Suddenly in my mind I heard a voice clearly saying, "There is one place you haven't looked". I knew immediately where to look – vertically above me! He was coming down in an almost vertical dive and laying off a perfect deflection. I kicked on right rudder and jerked my stick over in a steep starboard turn just at the moment that he opened fire. His tracer came so close to my aircraft that I ducked down in the cockpit to dodge the bullets. When this gambit didn't work they formed up and flew off. I returned to base without having fired a round, but also without a single bullet hole in my machine. A lucky escape as they had obviously been experienced pilots.

'A few days later, on 8 June, we were attacked by a mixed force of Macchis and 109s over the Cauldron area while on a Wing sweep. I was able to make a good quarter-front attack on a 109F which was attacking from the starboard side, but observed no result. I called for the rest of my section to reform on me, and while flying back east in line-abreast I saw a 109E flying west about 1,000 feet below us. Ordering my section into line-astern I swung down and delivered a quarter stern attack on him but did not get a good burst in owing to the speed at which I was closing. He stall-turned away and my Nos 2 and 3 attacked in succession without damaging him as far as I could judge. He again zoomed and stall-turned. I took a short cut, followed him down in his dive and then up in another zoom. As he again stall-turned I turned inside him and gave him a good burst. This time I saw tracer hit his engine and puffs of black smoke coming out of his cowling as he nosed forward into a shallow dive.

'I followed him down and, to my surprise, found that I was closing fast. I remember leaning forward to set the distance bars on my reflector sight to his exact wingspan – about 32

feet – as he was flying in a straight dive heading home, an absolute sitter. When he was exactly in range for a maximum concentration of fire, I pressed the trigger – Kittyhawks had a pistol grip like a revolver – *and not a gun fired!* I broke away to give my No 2 a shot but he could only fire a short burst before overshooting, and my No 3 had the same experience. By the time No 4 came in the 109E was low over enemy lines and my No 4 was frightened off by excellent light flak. This

was another man just not meant to die that day!

'Next day I was sent back to HQ Middle East for a spell of non-operational duties, and from July to September 1942 I ran an independent Operational Training Unit for the Turkish Air Force at Izmir (Smyrna) until a signal arrived from Ankara saying I was to return to Egypt as my application for transfer to the SAAF had been granted. I arrived back in Cairo aboard a Lodestar and was

Top: **Spitfire IX of 2 Squadron SAAF in Italy.**/*D. Bekker via M. Schoeman*

Above: **Retrieving the component sections of a crashed 5 Squadron SAAF Tomahawk, GL-P, AN420.**/*IWM*

interviewed at RAF HQ where I was offered immediate command of 94 Squadron if I was prepared to forego my transfer. I refused as 94 Squadron was at an all-time low in morale. Consequently on 15 October I was commissioned in the SAAF as a very junior Captain, and on the 21st rejoined No 2 Squadron as a supernumerary flight commander. Many of the oldtimers were still there but I quickly found out that I was out of touch with tactics as 2 Squadron was now functioning in a dual capacity – as fighters and as fighter-bombers.

'We were engaged on operations throughout the Alamein battle and some hectic engagements took place, but I did not make any claims. On 10 November 1942, however, while flying top cover for a Wing sweep over Tobruk, we spotted below two Bf109Es when west of Sollum. Leader Section turned after them but they evaded the attack. I therefore went down on one but could not turn with him due to the speed built up in my dive, so I pulled up again. I then saw the second 109E heading west low down. Putting my section into line-astern, we went after him, though this time I throttled back in my dive. As I was coming in on his tail he saw me and pulled his emergency boost; his aircraft literally jumped forward into a climb. I opened my throttle wide and caught him in the climb; he turned and I had a deflection shot at him. He

Right: **Tomahawk of 4 Squadron SAAF.**/*D. Bekker via M. Schoeman*

Below: **Major E. M. Baker and Lt W. A. Gillham in front of a 5 Squadron SAAF Kittyhawk III, 'H', already loaded with a 500lb bomb. In foreground a 1000lb HE bomb and ammunition boxes.**/*IWM*

half-rolled and I rolled with him, firing as I was on my back. He then went into a spiral dive and I followed him down firing as he came into my sights. Suddenly I saw the ground coming up fast and pulled out hard. I blacked out completely and waited for the impact, but as I greyed in I found myself flying straight and level between two big sand dune ridges, below the level of the ridge tops. I must have cleared the floor of the valley by no more than 20/30 feet at the bottom of the pull-out. Looking behind me I saw a column of smoke and flames where the 109E had gone in, and its destruction was confirmed by my No 2, Lt Quinn.

'My last combat occurred on 1 December when we spotted four aircraft bombing while on an offensive patrol over the Agedabia – Mir el Briga area south of Benghazi. We overhauled them rapidly and identified them as Macchi 200s. I attacked the leader and set him smoking but had to break away to avoid an attack by another Italian. I saw my No 3 attack the one I'd just damaged, obtaining a good hit. The Macchi pulled up in front of me in a left-hand turn and I again hit him with a deflection shot. I then swung in behind him and fired from dead astern. Almost simultaneously the pilot baled out, releasing his 'chute immediately. It fouled for a second then pulled clear but I think he must have caught my last burst.'

Below: **A 5 Squadron SAAF Kittyhawk IV being bombed up – highly adjacent to the squadron's temporary petrol dump!**/*K. Smy*

Bottom: **Spitfire Vc, ES172, WR-Z, of 40 Squadron SAAF.**/*via R. C. B. Ashworth*

Friday the 13th

While the American forces were later to make a huge contribution to the Allied efforts throughout the Middle East campaigns, many American citizens decided to join Britain's cause long before the USA officially came into the global conflict. One route to England was via Canada, where many individual Americans enlisted in the RCAF and thus made their way to an RAF front-line unit, thinly disguised as Canadians to avoid any legal breach of the USA's contemporary neutrality. One such 'Canadian' was Dick Halvorsen an American of Norwegian descent, who joined the RCAF, was posted to England and served briefly with

a Boulton Paul Defiant squadron, then in early 1942 arrived in the Middle East, posted to 213 Squadron to fly Hurricane IIs. The latter aircraft were, by that period, hopelessly out-classed by the Luftwaffe's Messerschmitt Bf109Fs and their (mainly) veteran pilots, but during the Gazala battles of May-June 1942 several DAF squadrons operated Hurricanes over the battle zone. One day in particular stands out in Dick Halvorsen's memory – 'Black Friday', 13 June 1942:

'That morning we had set out in a flight of six aircraft from 213's base at Gambut West, a distance south-westerly of where Rommel's Afrika Korps tanks were laying it on the British near Toburk. We had been sent up to thwart the Stuka dive-bomber attacks on Bir Hacheim where General LeClerc's Free French Army was beseiged by surrounding Italian and German artillery and infantry regiments. My reconstruction of the events of that day is based on a diary written for me by a chaplain in a hospital in Palestine, and follows the Bir Hacheim action where we dispersed the bombers and then headed back to base.

'We were just sauntering along at Angels 13 on our way home from the Stuka party over Bir Hacheim when I felt my Hurricane running rough at 2,600rpm and shoved the throttle up a bit to get back the effortless song of the Rolls-Royce Merlin engine. There was another cough and shudder and then I quickly switched over to the reserve tank, realising that since I'd just been in an air battle and was also acting as weaver, I was bound to be low on fuel. The song returned with a comforting pitch. It was the weaver's job, as Tail-End Charlie, to yaw and jink and zig and zag behind the formation, constantly throwing a roving eye into the rear-vision mirror and swivelling the neck to cover everything from directly abeam to astern, upwards and downwards. The formation leader took care of the other 180-degrees forward, but he flew straight and towards base, doing nothing evasive. The reason for the weaver's erratic flight was that the seat armour and tail assembly got in the way of rearward vision and *every* segment aft had to be covered to forestall an unexpected bouncing by enemy fighters.

Below: **Flight Sergeant Dick Halvorsen.**/*D. Halvorsen*

'Directly ahead and just slightly above me Blue One, Two and Three were in a tight, well-kept Vee but I noticed that Blue Five seemed to be falling behind. Blue Four wasn't around after the turkey-shoot on the Stukas and the ensuing dogfight with the top-cover Messerschmitts, and so the most optimistic view was that he'd failed to find us when Blue One ordered us to break off the fight and formate on him for the return home. I shoved the intercomm over to transmit and yelled, "Blue Five! Blue Five! Blue Six here. Pull up! Pull up! Formate! Formate!" Then I switched back to receive and got no answer. Something was wrong with his R/T, I guessed, and throttled back to give him coverage. I kept weaving. Then, with the suddenness of an apparition, there was a glint in the sky which I caught fleetingly in the mirror which was angled upwards. I gave my kite starboard rudder and looked over my shoulder and up, and saw more glints in the pellucid blue of the Libyan sky. They were no longer just glints, but taking shape as enemy mainplanes off which the fierce sun coruscated, and they were at about Angels 20 (20,000 feet). Had we been higher they would never have seen us, because we were headed south-easterly and the bright morning sun would have blinded their pilots to our position. This was instant knowledge, just as I *knew* they had spotted us as sitters unaware of them; that two-plus Bf109s were belting down at us for the kill; that our only hope was to turn tight to port and take advantage of the sun when the Jerries closed on us.

'By this time I'd switched R/T to transmit and was yelling, "Blue Leader – fighters on your tail – DUCK!" "Duck" was the signal for a left turn; "Aspidistra" for one to starboard. With your mouth full of cotton and adrenalin pounding towards your head, that second one is a hard tactic to mouth! I flung the switch back to receive, expecting instant acknowledgement and simultaneous action. The Vee ahead sailed on. I switched back to transmit and order the "Duck". Back to receive. No answer. No Flight reaction ahead. Blue Five hadn't answered me before and I'd thought *his* R/T had failed. Recollection came to me as I gave my Hurricane hard left rudder and pulled back hard on the control column – in the dogfight I'd felt something like a punch in the back and I now knew that it must have

Below: **Hurricane IIc, HL887, AK-W, of 213 Squadron at a secret LG *behind* enemy lines in November 1942. It was armed with only two of the more normal four 20mm cannons.**/*IWM*

been a shell that had wiped out *my* radio and been stopped by the seat armour.

'The tight turn was the Hurricane's only defence against a Messerschmitt's superior speed and overall manoeuvrability. For a breathless moment there's a sensation of a cannonball dropping from your throat to your anus and you momentarily black out. The weight of the weaponry in your wings had a lot to do with it, and hopefully you've had the foresight to switch the gunbutton from "Safe" to "Fire", and you're in a position to start negotiating with the enemy eyeball-to-eyeball. It's not the best stance for a confrontation but with four 20mm cannon at your thumb's command you command respect. When I'd completed my 180-degrees I flicked on my reflector sight, still set at close combat range – which I had a feeling was going to be appropriate. Now I could see four of them, two whom I'd not spotted coming from around eight o'clock high. I knew they'd focus their attention on me; it's tactically efficient to go for the straggler, the one who drops out of formation. By now Blue One might notice that Blue Five was lagging, and that the weaver was nowhere around.

'The Jerries were getting closer but my turn had upset their dive angle, taking me out of their sights. One whooshed past and, though I had nothing in my sights, I gave the cannons a split-second burst and a couple of tracers skedaddled crazily through the air, just to let them know I was alive and well. However, I wasn't exactly spoiling for a fight with the odds of four to one. All these 109s that had flashed past by now had red prop-bosses or spinners, indicating they were from another Gruppe than the yellow-spinnered ones we'd just been fighting. "Great", I thought, "all of them probably freshly fuelled and just sitting upstairs and waiting for us to return". The Germans were often methodical to a fault so that we could anticipate them, but this time they had pulled a switch. I just hoped that they had no hotshot pilot among the quartette. I wanted to stall long enough for Blue One or somebody to notice I was missing and come back with some aid and comfort.

'Hardly had I levelled out when I turned again; I couldn't just sit there depending on the weaver tactics and the mirror. I pulled back hard but sensed a lack of response in the rudder. I gave it hard left rudder when I straightened out and there was only a slight yaw, but in the mirror I saw an angled view of the rudder and bits of fabric fluttered from it. Quickly I looked forward and up. The Jerries had pulled up out of their initial dives, swung round, and were angling in twos from one o'clock and two o'clock. I canted left and lifted the nose, lining up my reflector sight for a 700-yard burst. The shots were off but an erratic tracer hit the wingman, and I got another burst in before I turned defensively, this time to the right. It was the correct move for the two o'clock bandits, who went by me a hundred yards away diving, but in my mirror I could see one of those I'd just fired at – had I damaged the other? I wasn't about to check on that – sitting behind and above me, and flashes came from his nose. Little holes like hemstitching appeared in my right wing and I turned left, losing something in the turn because of the holed wing and damaged rudder. She was as unresponsive as a sloop in stays, a mushy tub with no steerageway – she was a dying ship. The lack of response in the last turn told me my controls or cables had just been shot away.

'The manoeuvre hadn't done any good; the fighter was sticking to me like a band-aid, like a guy riding tandem on a bicycle built for two! I flipped the guard off the emergency gate and pulled for the extra zing I needed, then flicked right and down, knowing damn well it was useless but might buy some time for the Blue cavalry to show. I looked around the sky, eastward, but there weren't any friendlies, not even the sound of bugles! Another twist, and a cannon tracer went by and machine gun slugs hemstitched the right wing. Just a split-second burst; he was in no hurry. But where the hell are the other two?

'Suddenly a cannon shell hit the prop, right on the nose, just behind the spinner. Then another one hit, a few feet back of the first, then another, all in a line like a draughtsman's mechanical drawing. I sat transfixed, awed by the shooting accuracy, then in a split-second realised that with the spacing the next one should hit me in the back of the neck. For that fleeting moment I felt utterly serene – something I never experienced before or since. It had to be a split-second but seemed timeless, a fractional moment I was willing to trade for eternity. I loosened the harness in that moment and hit the lever to drop my seat, at the same time kicking desperately at the left rudder praying that this time something would somehow respond. Fantastically, it did and I yawed a little – the next shell went over my shoulder, still beautifully accurate, and hit just above the windscreen and burst into the reserve petrol tank just forward of the instrument panel. That did it. The explosive shell tore the tank apart and spilled flaming gasoline into the cockpit. Everything splashed wetly and then flamed, the whole cockpit an inferno. With my right hand I clawed at the harness release, awkwardly, desperately pulling the pin. It yanked free. I had no thought of my left hand, which was clutching the spade-grip of the stick, but I saw it was on fire. So were my longs (trousers) and desert shoes, and the fire crept onto my right hand and up to my tunic. By this time I was turning the aircraft over on its back and with the harness released I fell free, closing my eyes a second and counting, fearful that damn rudder might hit me, then I pulled the rip cord.

'Did they pack it right? A moment later I was reassured as the straps jerked at my crotch, and I looked quickly up from my swinging perch to make sure I wasn't dreaming. I saw my flaming aircraft heading downwards, then suddenly it exploded, the flames no doubt having raced through the vapour in the wing tanks and set off the belts of cannon shells in the wings. My first wild swings from the blossoming 'chute were slowing and I lifted my legs to smother some smouldering stuff on the knees of my trousers. Then I saw that in the upside-down bale-out I'd lost my shoes and socks. I looked at my hands and almost got sick and now knew better than ever why I'd called my gauntlets lucky.

'It was quiet up there at – what? – Angels 12? When I'd last looked at the altimeter it had read 13,000 on this Friday the 13th. I looked down and saw nothing but a mist of brown, and knew from experience that the promised *khamsin* (sandstorm) had arrived and was sweeping its sand across the desert. Then the quiet was broken by a rattle of gunfire and the pump-pump-pump of cannons, up around where I was. I found I was riding with my hands up – like a man surrendering – to keep the blood from rushing to them. I wasn't – or hadn't been – aware of pain moments back because terror had been a good counter-irritant. Now another fear made me forget them. Blue Section, what was left of it, had returned to take on the Jerries – no – the damn fools were circling me, far out and around, to ward off any attack on me.

'The Jerries kept hitting and running, diving in at the Hurris, and tracers were skittering around me, and I knew that plenty of GP armour-piercing stuff was peppering the air around me. All I needed was a tracer in my parachute and that would be it. "Get lost! Who needs you?", I mentally screamed at my mates, and maybe I even screamed it aloud. "You're damn near out of gas, you bloody idiots, and you'll never get back to base!" I saw one Hurricane break away seaward chasing a Messerschmitt, and then a second 109 following the Hurri. That left one 109 and he broke away as we got nearer the deck, and the rest of Blue Section headed south-easterly. I hoped they'd make it back.

'That one 109 wasn't gone long. I saw him whirl in a tight turn, gently extend it to a flat crescent, then come towards me. Was the bastard lining me up in his sights? I saw his flaps come down a bit, slowing him, in the distance, and had visions of his mainplane hitting me amidships, cutting me in two – real negative thinking. But he came past, throttle back, his goggles back off his forehead, and gave me a smile and then a thumbs-up followed by a wave – and if I could lip-read German, which I didn't understand, he seemed to be saying "Lots of luck". That was the way it was in the desert air war – *when* you had time for it. Lots of *noblesse oblige* – a little chivalry expended when you let somebody off the hook. The German pilot's final wave said, "So long, Alphonse", and my abortive wave back, "Auf wiedersehen, Gaston".

'Crazy. I began thinking of all that happened. A ringside seat from a parachute, free show to a dogfight. The kite blowing up, seconds after getting out. That last moment when the rudder functioned. I'd almost uttered the blasphemy, "Okay, JC, you've got control!" And then a silly thought, would the plane have exploded if I'd left the gun button on safe? Casuistical dilemma. I laughed. I must be going round the bend, really nuts. I was getting into the top billows of the *khamsin*, feeling the needles of sand on my feet. Funny I should have worn longs today – the first day ever. They saved my legs, but good. Why hadn't the bale-out fanned the flames instead of putting them out? My hands were hurting like hell but I didn't want to look at them again. Through the murk of the *khamsin* I saw stabs of orange and red on the deck – artillery? – tanks? I hadn't worn shorts because they were all mucked up with diarrhoea and we were still short-rationed on water. Today no diarrhoea – everything was "constricted", I guess . . .

'Suddenly the parachute caught in the *khamsin* and I was jerked like a puppet northwards. Almost lost the family jewels that time, and I tried to adjust the leg straps but my hand hurt too much. My vision adjusted to the brown twilight of the *khamsin* and I saw that I was getting close the ground and saw vague silhouettes. Tanks. A lot of them. All shooting. God! and I thought four cannons made a bloody racket! Knock off, chaps, I'm coming in on runway 00. Me in my bare feet and I could see the ground was chewed-up shale. Touch and roll, that was the only answer. All I needed for this one was flippin' leotards. My toes touched and I rolled *ballet bouffe* style, but the straps of the wind-filled parachute lifted me and slammed me down again, aggravating the back injury I'd got in a flip-over crash of a Defiant nightfighter back in Scotland. I tried to turn the scored wheel of the 'chute release but there was no skin on my hands so I couldn't get any purchase.

'Guns crashed all around me and there was a screech of metal as tanks moved ponderously on their treads of steel. There were vague silhouettes in the murk, moving, and others at a dead halt, on fire. My feet were taking a hell of a beating as I whipped through the battles, and my pants legs were in ribbons. I seemed to be coming out of the centre of the action, and suddenly saw a Bren gun-carrier, here where it was clearer, stop, change direction towards me, and presently overtake me. A couple of men leaped out and ran in my direction. One hurled himself across the shrouds of the 'chute, the other racing beyond him to stamp down and take the wind out of the 'chute. He gathered it up in a rumpled mass and walked towards me, and they both looked at me, puzzled, hesitating, maybe pitying, as I got to my feet. "You okay, mate?" one asked, the short one. It was a Scots accent and I saw now they were Scots Guards. I nodded and said, "Release the 'chute, will you?". Then I told them how to turn the knurled snap-lock, hit it, and then the straps dropped away. The tall one looked at my hands, then said, "Shall we take off them rubber gloves?". I looked at my hands, held shoulder-high against the blood-rush, and laughed. "Better leave it for the MO. That's skin, mate. The doc'll have to cut it away". The Bren gun-carrier was darting around us, its driver sensibly not stopping to provide a sitting target.

'Soon we were out of the angry, dust-whipping battle and clearing into relative sunshine, coming at last to an area where great tank-carriers sat, and busted-up tanks. An Italian Fiat CR42 suddenly whipped out of the sky, a fast biplane that did a dipsy-do over the area, flying real low and strafing everywhere. The tall Scot got him in his sights and held him in a long burst and swinging his gun, never letting up. The Eyetie pilot dropped his bombs in the open as Scotty's bullets ripped through his wings, then chewed away at his tail assembly, and the aircraft went out of control and hit somewhere over the dunes. You could see the black cloud slowly rising. I congratulated Scotty. "I wish we had all them bastards instead of that flippin' Rommel. He's tearing us to bits". A moment later we clanked up to a van with a Red Cross on it. Days later I was safe, in Palestine.'

Dick Halvorsen's opponent had been Oberleutnant Friedrich Körner of I/JG 27, the latter's 19th claimed victory. With a final tally of 36 credited victories, Körner was himself shot down on 3 July and became a prisoner. It was to be a further 30 years before the two former foes actually met. Halvorsen's personal account here was first published in his book *Steeds in the Sky* (Lancer Books, NY 1971) and is reproduced here with the author's permission.

Above left: **Friedrich Körner, Dick Halvorsen's chivalrous opponent.**/*Bundesarchiv*

Below: **Tame Junkers Ju 87D-1/Trop, ex-S7+LL of 33/St G3, used by 213 Squadron for amusement, hence the unit code markings denoting contemporary ownership.**

One of the Many

Aerial fighting has always attracted to itself an aura of glamour, a mantle of 'noble' combat, man to man, with a glittering fringe of knightly chivalry. Such an image was born mainly in the 1914-18 air warfare over France, and the leading 'aces' of all nations became national heroes, lauded and feted in the mass media of the period. This charisma extended to the fighter pilots of 1939-45, when high-scoring individuals became household names. Yet any objective study of the achievements of the fighter arms of every air force confirms unequivocally that the bulk of successes was gained by the 'silent majority' – that vast host of unsung, unpublicised fighter pilots who fought and, too often, died, playing an anonymous yet vital part in the ultimate victory. Sgt Alwyn Stephens was one such pilot; modest, unassuming, lowly in rank, just 'one of the many' who laid his life down in the cause of freedom. Unlike most pilots, Stephens maintained a series of private diaries recording his personal experiences, thoughts, feelings. Verbatim excerpts from those diaries are presented here to exemplify the day-to-day emotions and actions of an 'ordinary chap' – and as a tribute to all the other 'ordinary' fighter pilots who also made the ultimate sacrifice.

Leaving the UK by ship on 18 April 1942, Stephens disembarked at Takoradi, West Africa and a few days later was flown by Pan American Airways DC3 to Cairo. Here he spent nearly three months impatiently awaiting allocation to an operational unit, before joining 239 Wing a few miles west of Cairo in mid-August. A few days later he made his first solo flight in a Kittyhawk:

'I went up for my Kittyhawk solo; one hour of circuits and real bumps! I found taxying and take-off difficult due to the rudder position and brakes. Landing was all right but when the speed dropped there was a great tendency to swing in both directions at different times. Anyway, I survived.'

'On Thursday morning Fourneau and I ferried a Kitty each to Abu Sueir. On landing there my tailwheel just touched the ground when the whole thing ground-looped, ripping the undercart off, bending the prop, and generally buggering the whole bloody issue. I was cordially received and it was all taken in good part. We lunched in the mess there and spent the afternoon chatting with the engineering officer. We were finally picked up in a Lysander by Plt Off Cuddon. On the way home I fell asleep! On take-off from the RSU (Repair & Salvage Unit) we saw plenty of

Left: **Pilot Officer Alwyn C. Stephens (centre) snapped with two colleagues in Alexandria, 1942.**/*R. Stephens*

smoke and flames. Cuddon told us that Plt Off Moxly had come in to land and for some reason gone round again, on climbing his engine had cut and he had tried to turn back on the 'drome! Naturally he spun in. He was thrown clear, not too badly burned, but cut up quite a bit, and after a few hours he died. His lungs had been punctured by broken ribs, unfortunately.'

'I ferried a kite up to ALG (Advanced Landing Ground). I took off very late and was getting worried and desperate as the sun went down and determined to land at the very next 'drome. I did so and it proved to be LG97, the SAAF place. The adjutant received me extremely well and I dined in the officers' mess. After washing, the MO called in the adj's tent and took me into the mess and treated me to many beers. There he and I talked with a lieutenant about flying mainly until bedtime. There were some Americans there with Warhawks and they put a queer touch to the imperial SAAF mess! The South Africans all had that queer Oxford-Boer accent and all said "Ja", pronounced "Yaw", for "Yes". On Thursday morning I rose early and saw a sweep go off, and was surprised to hear that Jerry had been over the previous night. The beer inside me made me sleep soundly! I had breakfast in the mess again with American and SAAF officers and went out to my plane, watched the sweep come in, then took off for LG91, about ten miles away. Arrived there. Got in a truck with Fourneau and Vincent and off we went for base.

'11 September I started on my Italian grammar again, when some kites shot us up, coming very low over the Mess tent. Then we heard the popping of a Kitty engine cutting, ran out and saw a column of smoke on the 'drome, and assumed a kite had gone in. Then we saw that four Me109s had come over the mess, shot up the 'drome, destroying a Boston and Wellington and holing several aircraft. Then they shot up the wireless station and went down to Mene. I ran to my tent and got my camera out and took a photo of the smoke column. They also shot a Harvard down with a Sqn Ldr in it! He made a safe crash-landing.* I returned to my tent and put my camera away, and on coming out saw the Me's returning. Over the Mess two Hurricanes jumped them and shot one down. Some of our chaps went out and brought back a parachute, cannon shells and odds and ends. The pilot was taken by the army.† He baled out and was but slightly wounded. I heard another was shot down by Mene.

'27 September Gilbert and I were called down to fly once more. This time for a practice dogfight. I decided not to risk a formation take-off, so I started quickly and taxied out. The wind for a change was in the opposite direction, so I had the whole length of the 'drome to taxi, and I had to go slowly as a kite taxied out from R & D Flight in front of me. I followed him, let him take off, then ran up and tested my switches, and when I turned to take off there was a prang on the 'drome and burning too! I decided that the chap in front of me had spun in, and so I took off – just over the Watch Hut too. Just as I was going to put my wheels up I saw a queer-looking kite in front of me at about 1,000 feet, with clipped wings. I decided it *must* be a Mustang – but I had my doubts! Then, looking to my right, I saw bags of flak! Then in a flash my worst

thoughts were confirmed. I turned into a steep diving turn to the left, put my wheels down again, another turn, and I landed – all in a few minutes! And what a landing – it was perfect! The burning kite was a Boston, shot down on the circuit, injuring the crew of three, one of whom was an erk cadging a ride.* The chap in front of me was White and he took off while the 'drome was being strafed the first time; and I took off when they strafed for the second. Willmott, up on a test, got behind one and found his guns not working, and two SAAF in Tommies (Tomahawks) up at 10,000 feet did not see a damn thing!'

Late in September Stephens finally obtained a posting to operations, joining 250 Squadron, flying Kittyhawks.
'1 October The third detail was vectored onto a badly escorted Stuka party. Barber (Flt Lt M.C.H.) got three! They dropped their bombs on their own troops, and altogether eight were destroyed and many more damaged and probable. In the mess in the evening everyone was getting drunk. A bunch of 112 Squadron chaps came over, Bobby Sale amongst them. Ben Curphy came too, with a 109 confirmed. Fourneau and a few from 450 Squadron came over. Their Mess was down as they were all posted to base to chase away the 109s.'
'I feel these Kittyhawks are good operationally, but the Allison engine is bugger-all good. So many crashes have come about, and so many planes have burst into flames. I intend in the future taking every precaution. I shall take up no kite that I am not satisfied with. I learn a new lesson from each friend of mine that is killed, and at each death I feel more bitter.'
'6 October I went up in battle formation the first time and again for close formation. At 1.0 (1 o'clock) we were on readiness, and at 2 we took off, six of us as top cover for 3 RAAF Squadron, and the six I was with as top cover for 112 Squadron bombing El Alamein. It was an uneventful trip for us, except over the target we encountered inaccurate flak, about 700 feet below and about 500 in front. We remained over the target for about two minutes and then went home, diving from 12,000 and reaching 2,000 over base. The landing was odd. We usually land in echelon left, and I turned to find them landing echelon right, so I had to go through three slipstreams to land, hitting the third about 20 feet above the ground – I made a good landing anyway.'
'7 October I was put down for the second detail on Wednesday morning. After spending my time in the mess, and ferrying a new kite from the ACOs, we took off at 13.00 with 500-pounders on. We managed it comfortably

* Shot down by Uffz Gruber, III/JG 27.

† Fwbl Fink, III/JG 27, shot down by Flt Lt Lawrence and Sgt Campbell, 127 Sqn.

* Of 24 SAAF Sqn, shot down by Bf109s of III/JG 53, led by Leutnant Jürgen Harder.

69

Above: **Tomahawk casualty from 250 Squadron, August 1941.**

with flap. Weaving was difficult on the way there, but when the dive came I was so confused and excited that I did not even see what I was bombing! I just dropped the damn thing and ran. I felt three blows behind me. Very probably bombs exploding, though the ack-ack was very intense and accurate. We came back weaving and diving gently. I was lagging a good bit on that. I made a very bumpy landing, very near the prang on the field, and that nearly made two. Anyway, I taxied back safely.'

'*20 October.* On Tuesday morning I spent my time cleaning out the tent and drying out my kit. Then a big Daba show went out, and I went up to Amriya for a very cold shower. On returning the show came back, and Roberts was missing. During the afternoon I went out on a bombing show. We went out with 112, escorting bombers, to Fuka and as we approached Daba we broke off and went in and bombed a dispersal. 112's bombs went on the 'drome, but ours went right into the dispersal. 112 ran away and left our A flight in the shit. Taylor was lost. We returned fast and furious. Today 450 have lost two, 112 one, and we two. Only one Me109 destroyed confirmed on the wing. Not so good. But the bombers have certainly done good work. So far the squadron has lost four since I have been here. That is good by ordinary standards, but bad by ours.'

'*30 October.* On Friday (30th) I did nothing much except get paid in the morning until I went off on the second detail, escorting Mitchells over Fuka. This was my first show as far west as that. On the way back,

approaching Daba, I was jumped by two 202s (Macchis) but Steward, my No 1, spun on turnabout and I followed him down. As we pulled out of the dive he squirted at a 109 and we turned into the sun for the return attack, and we both opened up as a figure came out of the glare – but discovered to our horror that it was an American! After a few turnabouts we caught and rejoined our formation. On landing we were informed that Air Chief Marshal Tedder was arriving in 15 minutes. I ran and shaved and came back to find him in the mess. He talked to Judd* and the Wingco and invited and asked many questions. During that time the 'phone rang and Ginge Taylor answered, and told whoever it was to ring back again as the Air *Vice*-Marshal was there! It was a hell of a "black" and surreptitious grins flitted around the faces in the Mess.'

'On Saturday I got up late, but was up on the second detail by 10 o'clock. We were medium cover to B-25s over Fuka. 450 Squadron were below and the Americans' Warhawks above. Over the target I saw a formation of nine-to-twelve Macchis dive into the Americans. Later I found out there were "15-plus" of which they got three confirmed and three probables. Some of those 202s came down into our formation, and Russell, my No 1, turned time and time again into them to drive them off. One, diving fast away from the Americans, came at 90° to me. I started to turn into him but he went by so fast and so close I *heard* him. Another came down on us and Russell spun on the turnabout, so I went over

* Sqn Ldr M. T. Judd, then OC 250 Squadron.

on my back and dived out after him. Then we made after the formation and saw three 202s behind us, and turned on them. They climbed, two close together and one lagging, so we both attacked and fired at him, seeing no results. On breaking off the engagement I turned to look behind me only to see and feel the fire of a 202. I dived instantly. I had a shell in each wing, bullets in the port wing, two on either engine bank, five ricochets off my starboard front perspex, and one in the belly which blew open my fuselage hatch, and put my receiving set and sundry other gadgets u/s. Oil and glycol poured from the port bank and, Russell leading, we headed for the Depression (Qattara). I had full boost and revs, open wide radiator, and my ASI (Air Speed Indicator) was shot away. I called R but got no answer (naturally – one set u/s).

'We reached ground level before getting to the Depression and we dived over the edge to the ground some 300ft below. By then my engine was losing power and my petrol was low in all tanks. I ran one tank dry and could not change it over without great difficulty; that scared me. My eye was ever on the temperature and pressure gauges; my one fear was fire, for I was too low to bale out. By that time all the perspex on the port side was covered in oil. Over the R/T I made R. understand I was low in petrol and had no ASI. We came to LG 37 and then my engine began to miss on the port cylinders, and the fuel warning light flickered with ten indicated gallons in the reserve tank. The wheels would not pump down and, losing height and speed fast, I could not use the emergency system.

Thankfully, the flaps came down, and by formating on Russell I made a crash-landing. The engine was so clapped out I had to use 35 inches of boost for the "landing" run! After grating along the ground the plane took off again. I flung my arms around my head and braced myself, and the plane landed sideways in a cloud of sand. I thanked Russell afterwards and he refuelled and flew home. I signalled Wing and asked for transport. It was

Above: Scene at Sorman/Zavia in July 1943.

Right: **Wg Cdr F. E. Rosier DSO, (later, AM, Sir Frederick).**/*IWM*

promised but never came until next day. I spent the afternoon and evening with 127 Hurricane Squadron – we had a colossal piss-up and dirty sing-song!'

'*6 November.* On Saturday morning (6th) we were up before dawn and had orders to go beyond LG106 to 115 near Sidi Haneish. There were only three vehicles, the two flight trucks and the staff car. The trip to El Alamein was uneventful. After that we came into the battle region. On both sides of the road were German vehicles and tanks blown up and burned out. Shell cases and ammo boxes were strewn everywhere, and corpses black with age lined up for burial. The battle was five days old when we passed by. Some of the German dead in this area had mines attached to them, and our burial parties consequently suffered casualties. We saw many of our vehicles too, with wheels blown off by German mines. We stopped at several trucks for loot and picked up rifles and ammunition. We stopped at what turned out to be a German Div HQ. We picked up papers and pay books for the I0 (Intelligence Officer), and Wally Tribken found a Luger. We drove on to Daba from there and lunched at LG 20, where we examined a Ju 88 and several Bf 109s, all of which had been rendered up though they looked repairable to me. One looked as if it had only just had an engine change. The old one lay beside it with a cannon shell through it. We fired our rifles there and ate some Jerry ration biscuits we found in a box.'

'As we passed the other Daba 'dromes we saw pranged 109s, 88s, and even Wellingtons. We saw some gliders too. At this point was the biggest concentration of vehicles ever, for it was here that the panzers were trapped without fuel or oil. We were pleased to see the

result of our strafing in the burned-out skeletons of trucks and conveyors. At intervals we came across scattered graves, but there were some organised graveyards. We stopped at an Italian HQ full of personal kit. It was covering an area of about two square miles! The unfortunate owners were herded on the opposite side of the road. There must have been about 2000 prisoners there. Already we had seen trucks full of Italians going towards the PoW camps. Some trucks were driven by Italians and had no guard at all. Some prisoners were even thumbing their way back!

Most were smiling though some looked miserable. After we passed Fuka the road became blocked and muddy. Being a small party, we were able to leave the road at congested points, though the risk of mines was great. Where we cut across the peninsula to Sidi Haneish the mud became worse, and in parts the road was completely under water. We saw a Bren gun-carrier almost completely submerged on the side of the road, its crew standing by boiling water for tea, looking very miserable in the rain. We even saw a Sherman bogged, though not for long. Approaching Sidi Haneish the ground became higher and not so boggy. We saw in one area, not an aerodrome, eight burned out CR 42s, five of them in a straight line a hundred yards apart, but so far not a single 202 was pranged.

'We were within an hour's travel of LG 115 when we stopped for the night. The Jerries had fled so hastily they left an entire camp behind without even burning anything, so we spent the night there. We got up at dawn on Sunday and ate some German bully and biscuits and made some tea that West provided. Then we pushed on 'til we came to 013 and learned that the two roads to LG 115 were impassable; one was bogged and the other mined. 013 being rich in prangs, we decided to stop there and await orders – God

knows where from! On the 'drome were He IIIs, Ju 88s, 109s, and over a dozen Stukas. I obtained a very nice compass from a Stuka. We finally settled down by the wind-sock. The trucks were sent for petrol and the staff car for food. Wg Cdr Rosier landed in a Hurricane and told us that the Americans had landed in North Africa, and that church bells were ringing in England. He also told us that Mersa Matruh was in our hands, and we were to stay while he returned to Group to get orders for us. Later on 601 Squadron turned up and one of their lorries was blown up by a mine, just where we'd been looting – it shook me! The staff car failed to find food but Jerry Warman scrounged some from an army unit. We had a bit of cheese and piece of bread and syrup each. Water was low so we had a ration of tea. Later, a Maggie (Magister) landed and we were told to go to LG 101, another 'drome nearby.

'After that news came through from Wing and "other sources" that we were going to move on to LG 76 near Sidi Barrani, and our B convoy was passing the bottom of our branch road, and we had to meet it. So we went down and met 112 Squadron on the way. They were camping there for the night before going on to LG 76. We "dined" with them that night. Bully was the dish, and being so hungry we

Above: **Fish out of water. 'Sharkmouth' Kittyhawk ET789, GA-C of 112 Squadron which Sgt Hogg force-landed at El Daba on 12 September 1942 after a fight with a Bf109. Hogg was shot down again on 21 October 1942 and became prisoner of war.**/R. A. Brown

Above: **Fed-up and far from home. 601 Squadron Spitfire EP455 and its well-tanned pilot on 'Standby' duty.**

really did enjoy it. Next morning we had breakfast with 112 and set out before them. The road to Mersa Matruh was littered with strafed vehicles and tanks, all burned out, and Matruh itself showed black scars of fires and heavy bombing. We took the inland road to Barrani and this was very clear indeed. We passed nothing. Even the abandoned stuff was absent. We caught up with Sqn Ldr Strawson, who had trouble with his vehicle, so we stopped, mended his engine, had tea, and fired off our guns. We heard heavy firing in the distance. We took it to be our naval big guns battering Barrani. Then some trucks came racing towards. us. They were a refuelling party who'd gone ahead of us and had met Jerry! We were ahead of our armoured cars, for a few minutes later the armour plus a brigadier arrived on the scene and refuelled from the bowsers. We started back then for a track that would take us to LG 76 or 75. Sqn Ldr Strawson now told us to go to 75 instead of 76 – that made a total of four aerodromes we had been posted to and not arrived at.'

'We picked up two prisoners; an Italian of about 40 in the Red Cross, and a fairly young German very smart and military. Soon after a couple of Me 109s came down and strafed us. We drew off the road and ran for the shelter of a sand dune. The poor Italian was terrified and started to dig himself in like a rabbit. The German was only shaken a little. Later on when we came to our desert track we dropped them and gave them water and a can of bully. The Jerry appreciated that and saluted us. We saw nothing on the way to LG 76 for the land

was stony and undulating. We passed an ancient pranged Kitty I, and a very much bombed and bug-eaten railway station. We ate and camped for the night at LG 76 – so far we had been posted to LGs 106, 115, 101, 75 and 76 – and all in four days!'

Once the whole squadron was together again, a few strafing sorties were flown, then late in November came leave in Cairo, followed in December by attachment to 53 RSU for non-operational 'rest' duties. Celebrations were widespread – mainly on 'liberated' Italian wine and beer flown in from Egypt – and Christmas provided the traditional Service festivities:

'On Thursday (24 December) I spent the afternoon in my tent reading. At 4.30 we got paid and at six o'clock we started the Christmas drinking session. At 7.30 the padre conducted a carol sing-song and we all attended and it went on until nine. The drinking in our mess was stupid, and a chap who thought he could sing tried to – I went to bed. On Christmas morn I got up early and moved my kit over to the Jerry tent; our EPI being wanted to provide part of the airmen's mess. At noon all officers and sergeants served dinner to the airmen, and when it was over we retired to the mess and listened to the King's speech before having our own feast. During our evening drinking the Americans and a bunch of our own ground crew gate-crashed us and things became unpleasant. They had finished all their own drink and were trying to finish ours. I went to bed and left them to it.'

In January 1943 came a return to 250 Squadron and by mid-month Stephens was back on operations:

'*14 January*. I was on the late morning show on Thursday, escorting bombers over Bir Dufan. Just before reaching the target I lost Holmes, my No 1. The R/T panic was colossal. There were Messerschmitts reported all over the place and I could not see them. In a turnabout I lost the formation, joined a 450 Squadron type and lost him in a tussle, and finished up with the 3 SAAF close cover. I followed the bombers back and finally landed with two tanks drained and one nearly empty. We lost Webster and Kirkman, and eleven were lost from the whole show. 3 SAAF lost five of them, including Gibbes,* and two later in the day. That day the Kitty Wing lost 22!'

Two days later Stephen's back-dated promotion to flight sergeant was promulgated. '. . . I got up late on Sunday and went to the Orderly Room to enquire about back pay, and was delighted to learn that my crown was back-dated five months.' Next day, Monday,

* R. H. M. Gibbes, who returned to his unit six days later.

18 January: 'Getting up before dawn, we took off as soon as it was light, leading 3 (SAAF Sqn) and 260 (Sqn) who were on top. Nearing Tarhuna, we bombed MT just as we met some 109s. One was shot down by the Wingco (Wg Cdr H. F. Burton). It later turned out that the 109s were escorting 12 Stukas, who were seen by 260 Sqn.' Within a week the Axis retreated from Tripoli towards the Tunisian border.

'I got up at dawn on Sunday and packed my bed roll and we were soon on our way. On the way to Tarhuna, via Beni Ulid, we saw many destroyed Italian and German tanks. In one place we saw 11 vehicles nose to tail, burned out. Strafing was in evidence all the way along the route. We paused for lunch at Tarhuna. We were at Castel Benito by 3.30. Only a few of the bridges on the way were blown up. One had a time bomb under it – it blew up some time after we had crossed it. After settling myself in a tent, I took a walk around the 'drome. Apart from much burned wreckage of aircraft, there were about forty G-50s, MC 200s and 202s, SM 79s, and all sorts of Italian light aircraft. One graveyard must have covered three acres, all Ju 52s and German craft. The hospital, officers' quarters, hangars, stores etc were all full of loot. The evening in

Below: **'Ye Olde Messerschmitt Inn' – crews of a Kittyhawk squadron utilise the tail section of a Messerschmitt Bf110 for their unit 'booze bar'.**/*via B. H. A. Playford*

the mess there was much talk of Tripoli and billets.' Next day: 'A house had been found for our mess and a Chianti distillery found! 3 Squadron sent up a bowser and filled up from a vat! There were vats there 15 feet across and as many feet deep, full of wine. People streamed in from all quarters and filled up Jerrycans and all sorts of things. That night the squadron got drunk to a man – in our tent we finished up with a soup brew.'

'*26 February.* We bombed Gabes West and the top squadrons and our top cover were jumped. We saw no e/a (enemy aircraft) but from the show Collier and Nitz didn't return. On the second show there was no action. I sat around the mess the while until the third show, when we bombed Bordj Touz. Stone and I fought a 109, got separated and I came back unknowingly along the Mareth Line! No wonder I collected so much flak. Stone saw me in the distance, a cloud of black smoke! I got in three squirts, two of which were good ones. On return we found that Collier and Nitz were back, having landed at Ben Gardane. Nitz had a destroyed and Collier two damaged. Gordon Troke came in late without his No 2, a young New Zealander on his second op. Gordon got one probable. There was Chianti in the mess after dinner and I got stewed.'

'*1 March.* At dinner dozens of Spits came in and landed from 244 Wing. It turned out they were very suddenly shelled and took off under fire!* Bags of panic, consequently we were on readiness, bombs on, bombs off, tomorrow at six – no, 6-30 – oh Hell! Ops can't make up their minds.'

A few days later the squadron moved onto Tunisian soil: 'At last we are on Tunisian soil and I feel more confident than ever. The news has just come through that Jerry has gone back to the Mareth Line leaving 50 tanks behind. The air here is very invigorating and I spent the morning outside doing odd jobs around the tent. The tent is situated in a little wadi covered in camel thorn, and many herbs that I've not encountered before. One herb smells of celery and tastes very much like it.'

Friday, 26 March. 'Our team was at 40 minutes all Friday morning. The Yanks came to operate from our 'drome and amongst them was 'Mac' Powers, now a flight leader awaiting his captaincy! The AOC came and personally briefed all pilots on the big strafing show. It was to be a nonstop bomb and strafe of the troops opposing the New Zealanders. He was very rude and callous about the whole thing. Bill West and Browning did not return from the first show. Bruce Cole was wounded in the knee, and the CO was hit. There are seven

missing from the Wing. There were so few kites serviceable for the second show that I did not get off'.

'*Monday, 29 March.* Up early Monday. We took off at 6.20. The Jerry is in full retreat north of Gabes and we were to bomb and strafe the road continuously all day. Squadrons went out at 15-minute intervals and bombed and re-armed immediately on return, and came to readiness as soon as possible. The squadron did five shows and I got two in.'

'*Sunday, 4 April.* We moved our dispersal *(the squadron had moved over the Mareth Line to El Hamma the day before)*. As we were erecting our tent, four Fw 190s bombed and strafed us with six 109s as top cover. Two were killed and a few wounded. By lunch we were settled in again but at 2 o'clock we were bombed again. Flamers were scored on the road both times. These Jerries are good but I think they'll taste their own medicine tomorrow. Leo Hutt returned from his liquor scrounge with nine bottles. Everyone is feverishly digging slit trenches now. Wing is being shelled, though so far there have been no casualties. Gurkhas have been sent after the guns. We all got drunk on Leo's very good wines and liqueurs.'

'*El Djem. Sunday, 18 April.* At 4.45 I took off on another Ju 52 sweep, seeing nothing, and landed at dusk. The Yanks got 81 destroyed!! Up late on Monday, I spent the

* At Hazbus Main airfield.

76

morning unpacking. The SAAFs got 15 destroyed! In the late afternoon we were briefed for a Ju 52 show and took off at 5.30. We saw nothing and landed by flarepath.'

'On Thursday morning (6 May) the Tunis action commenced. With 800 guns, two armoured Divs, two infantry Divs, and the Guards Brigade all on a six-mile front – the army push. 108 bombers with a squadron each escort, and Spits covering the lot, went over in a space of 14 minutes! The other side (1st Army) supplied as many, all to bomb the one road to Tunis. In the evening I went off on a show, bombing that same road. MT was tightly packed on it, in full retreat. We landed at dusk.'

'*8 May.* Off on a show after lunch, we bombed a ship outside Tunis harbour. Weather was foul. When we returned, Tunis had fallen!'

'*10 May.* On Monday I read in the Mess until lunch-time, when we did a bomber escort. Six of us escorted 18 bombers over to Pantelleria. Altogether there were 108 bombers, 36 P-40s, 24 Spit Vs and some Spit 9s.'

After the fall of Tunis came leave until the end of the month, and during this time Stephens was commissioned as a pilot officer. Wing training towards the projected invasion of Sicily followed the leave period.

'*22 June.* Up early on Tuesday. We went to Sorman by truck early and spent the morning lining the kites up. The King (HM King George VI) inspected us at 9.30, accompanied by Broadhurst and Monty. We flew back by 12. I bathed all afternoon and spent the evening writing letters in the mess. The King's inspection was pretty hopeless. The cheering was feeble, and he drove round in a car and didn't even say anything to us.'

'*10 July.* On Saturday 10th, I heard that Sicily was invaded! I waited all day for the call for me to go to Malta (where his squadron had moved days earlier). It didn't come. I read nervously all day. Early on Sunday morning I was called and, without breakfast I flew to Malta with a mixed formation. Arrived there, I broke fast in the officers' mess and put my kit in the billet. All day was spent in the dispersal on the 'drome. An unsuccessful op was pulled off and I was on the next team. Finally at 6.30 we took off and did an armed recce as far as Catania. Catania is in flames. The sea is full of craft of all sizes from barges to liners. The beaches are crammed with troops and craft.'

This was the last diary entry. On 12 July 1943, Alwyn Stephens and his wing-man collided in mid-air whilst on a sortie over Sicily. The wing-man managed to bale out. Alwyn Stephens failed to return . . .

Artistry

Above: FIFI – a 239 Wing
Kittyhawk's nose
adornment./Dr F. T. Pearce

Left: Deadly teeth. Sharkmouth
unit marking of 112 Squadron
RAF circa September 1941.
Second aircraft is AK461,
'A'./R. A. Brown

Above: No Orchids (ie 'for Miss Blandish') on the cowling of P-40N, OK-O of 450 Squadron RAAF at Vasto, early 1944./*via* F. F. Smith

Left: A wasp painted over the centre-roundel of a Hurricane, believed to be of 213 Squadron RAF.

Left: **Tomahawk** *Hepsa-Bah* **of 3 Squadron RAAF.**/*IWM*

Right: **260 Squadron Hurricane nose decoration, 1941.**/*M. Gidman*

Left: **Neville Duke and his 92 Squadron Spitfire, suitably adorned with his claims for nine German and ten Italian victories.**

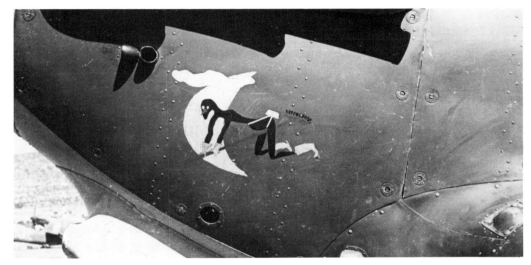

Above left: Marjorie – **Kittyhawk CV-Z of 3 Squadron RAAF.**/*via F. F. Smith*

Below: **The personal insigne of Lance Wade, a Texan serving with 33 Squadron in its Hurricane period.**/*IWM*

Left: Snifter – **a national Australian cartoon figure of the period carried on Kittyhawk AK951, CV-O of 3 Squadron RAAF in 1943.**/*via F. F. Smith*

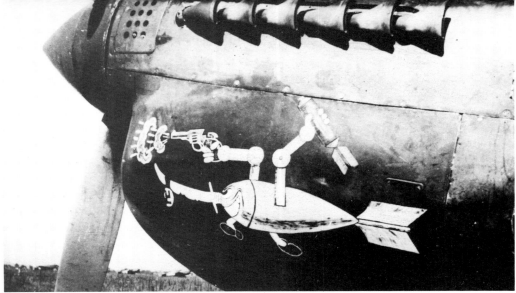

Left: **Mechanical 'beastie' decorating a 3 Squadron RAAF Kittyhawk (CV-V) at Cutella, Sicily in late 1943.**/*via F. F. Smith*

Right: **The five-pointed star of the USAAF, prominent on a Warhawk of the 65th FS, 57th Fighter Group.**/*IWM*

Left: **Curtiss P-40F of the 64th FS** (*Black Scorpions*) **of 57th FG and its cynical label,** *Messerschmitt Bait.*/*via F. F. Smith*

Left: **Sqn Ldr R. H. M. 'Bobby' Gibbes DSO, DFC of 3 Squadron RAAF and his aptly-marked Tomahawk.**/*IWM*

Below: **A magnificently winged leopard (?) beautified the nose of this SAAF Tomahawk.**/*IWM*

Above: **Fighting Aussie kangaroo on a 450 Squadron RAAF Kittyhawk at Foggia, 1944.**/*via F. F. Smith*

Below: **Baltimore V, FW332, 'R', named** *Redwing* **and with an 80-sortie log recorded on its** nose section, which belonged to 232 Wing, 1944-45./*IWM*

Right: **Sqn Ldr M. P. Nash, commander of 3 Squadron RAAF in 1945, by the tail of Mustang KH714, CV-P at Foggia.**/*via F. F. Smith*

Beau belles

'No 600 (City of London) Squadron of the Auxiliary Air Force effectively joined the Desert Air Force when we flew to Malta from Bone, in Tunisia, on 25 June 1943. But the story of how we came to be selected for this posting is perhaps worth a line or two. In support of the invasion of French North Africa, we had been successively under Eastern Air Command and North-West African Coastal Air Force. We were one of the three nightfighter Beaufighter squadrons in the Algeria-Tunisia theatre. We were a self-contained unit, complete with our own cooks and butchers, equipment and postal clerks et al – given sources of fuel, food, and ammunition and oxygen – and could move around at will. As the First and Eighth Armies chased the Afrika Korps into Cape Bon, we settled down for a while at the battered and mosquito-ridden Bone airfield.

'At about this time our extremely shrewd CO, Wing Commander 'Paddy' Green – originally of 601 Sqn, AAF – got the 'buzz' that only one of the three Beaufighter squadrons would go across to the Desert Air Force for the invasions of Sicily and Italy; the other two would remain in North Africa to defend Algiers, Tunis and the other ports.

This second-line role appealed to him not at all! Sensing that the Air Staff at Algiers were unlikely to part with what they thought was their best squadron, he proceeded – to the despair of Alfie Clennett, his first-class Engineer Officer – to send in aircraft serviceability returns which reflected neither the true situation nor credit on the squadron. This went on for some weeks and then – bingo – 600 was nominated for the Desert Air Force. I often wonder if the guys at Algiers ever became aware of this little stratagem.

'At once, a total transformation. Our quite splendid ground crews, many of whom were original pre-war Auxiliaries, worked flat out. New aircraft with sand-coloured camouflage flowed from the storage depots and were given stringent acceptance checks and thorough air tests. The tired old grey-green aircraft were polished up and flown away. We had a deadline to make in Malta and, thanks to "Chiefy" Nelson and his boys, we made it.

'After an exhilarating wave-top flight to Malta, we settled into our battle-scarred dispersal at Luqa, each aircraft in its own blast pen of soft yellow stone and rubble-filled petrol cans. The island was bulging with aircraft, ships, equipment and men. The Luqa

Left: **600 Squadron crew members at Cassibile in August 1943. From left: Sgt Phil Rose, navigator to Lt Harry Newton; Flt Lt Laurie Dixon DFC, nav to Desmond Hughes; Fg Off Reg Gillies DFC, nav to Wg Cdr Green (OC Sqn); Flt Lt Desmond Hughes DFC (now AM, Sir), author of this chapter.**

Above: **Wg Cdr C. P. 'Paddy' Green DSO, DFC commander of 600 Squadron, in the cockpit of his Beaufighter at Cassibile, August 1943. Below his navigator, Reg Gillies, paints on a swastika for their eighth victory by night.**

Below right: **Now thrive the armourers . . . erks of 600 Squadron preparing a Beaufighter for night ops; tending and cleaning 20mm cannons and checking the engines.**

officers' Mess was full so we were billetted in the Meadowbank Hotel in Sliema – a sharp contrast to our tented camps in Africa. Everyone seemed still to be celebrating the raising of the long siege. Food and drink were plentiful and the fare and service at the Union Club were remarkably good. Or was it just our relief from soya links and canned M & V?

'Luqa was commanded by Group Captain (now ACM) 'Willie' Merton, and our stay there was very happy. Air Marshal Sir Keith Park, driving his red MG sports car, was one of our first visitors. The airfield was in astonishingly good condition considering the pounding it had received, though the sheer drop off the end of the runway into a quarry was somewhat daunting. The fighter controllers – such as Roger Frankland, Lawrence Brown and Bill Pratley – knew their stuff and had our confidence. Brownie and Pratley were due to go ashore with their mobile GCI radars very shortly after H-hour. The Luftwaffe now scarcely ever approached the island even by night, so our nights were fairly uneventful as we brought our aircraft up to peak efficiency. Sadly, I did have a distant view of the shooting down of a Wellington by a German nightfighter off Sicily.

'On 10 July, Sicily was invaded and 600's "purple patch" began. The Luftwaffe showed up in agreeable numbers over the beaches and as our GCIs got ashore and deployed – which they did with remarkable speed – we inflicted heavy casualties on them. Twenty-five bombers were destroyed in the first week; the most successful crews being Paddy Green and Reg Gillies with seven (including four in one patrol) and Flt Lt John Turnbull, RCAF and Sgt Fowler, who notched up six. I was content enough with two. The morale of the squadron rocketed to new heights and the rivalry between the crews to get the most favourable slots in the night flying programme was intense. Over 1000 hours were flown in a month, a high figure for defensive nightfighters.

'On 25 July, 600 moved to Cassibile, just south of Syracuse, where we stayed for two months. The Sappers had made a magnificent airstrip, long and smooth, cut clean through a

large almond and orange plantation. The only problem was that it lay very close to the Syracuse anchorage and our dusk patrols were fired on by the ships every night as we took off and climbed away. We protested vigorously to the Navy but they swore blind that they were being attacked by Ju 88s. It was not until Flt Lt Raleigh Hilken's aircraft was hit by a 20mm Oerlikon shell – happily, not an HE one – that the Navy believed us; and then only because we plonked the offending shell on the

local Captain's desk. Paddy Green and I were immediately offered pink gin and a shower, which we were glad to accept. Oddly, the chief culprit proved to be a converted cross-channel ferry in which I had travelled many times before the war between Belfast and Liverpool!

'At Cassibile it was back to tents and, as always, the various paths through the camp were named after famous thoroughfares in the City (London) – Moorgate, Cannon Street, Eastcheap, and so on. The heat in the middle

Above: **Major inspection on a Beau at Edcu, March 1943.** / *K. G. Thomas*

Below left: **Warrant Officer Yorke and one of his armourers on 600 Squadron check out a pair of .303 Browning machine guns, while another 'plumber' services a rifle in his bench vice.**

of the day was intense and the ground crews had to be careful not to touch the aircraft with their bodies as they worked stripped to their shorts; it was only too easy to lose a large expanse of skin. Our MO, Peter Scurlock, was intrigued to find that cuts and burns suffered at Cassibile were very difficult to heal, yet dried up within a couple of days when people went elsewhere – some odd effects of volcanic dust from Etna?

'We continued to provide night cover for the forward ports and airfield and, though the intensity of German night bomber operations fell away as the Allied armies swept northwards, there were moments of intense excitement. One such happened on the night of 11 August when a determined attack, mainly with incendiaries, was made on the day fighter airfield at Gerbini, near Catania. At last I was on patrol at the right time and, with very accurate GCI control, was put in AI contact with four Ju 88s – which obligingly flew in nicely-spaced intervals. With three of these, masterly directions from my navigator, Fg Off Laurie Dixon, brought visual contact and one bomber after another fell to the devastating punch of the Beaufighter's four cannons and six machine guns. The fourth Ju 88 we followed into the AA fire zone and, as we closed in, I found we were collecting all the unpleasantness intended for the enemy bomber. When I started to *hear* the shell-bursts and some fragments rattled off us, I decided that discretion was the far better part of valour and broke away before visual contact. My aircraft was slightly damaged but how much was due to "flak" and how much to debris from the destroyed bombers was not clear.

'Six nights later an odd incident occurred. I was on the last patrol, due to finish shortly after dawn. There had been no "trade" and I was winging my way back to Cassibile at first light when the controller said that something had just shown up moving north off Syracuse, fairly low. He positioned me so that this target would be silhouetted against the dawn glow in the east. To my astonishment, I saw a Ju 87 Stuka, not at all a target we expected to meet at that period. I swung in to intercept but the Stuka crew saw me before I could close to firing range. He immediately whipped into a steep turn to the left. I yanked the Beau – not exactly an agile aircraft – around after it, thinking to myself that this was going to be one helluva turning match, and fired a quick two-seconds' burst. This was mainly to impress the rear gunner who was already firing at us. I saw no strikes from this burst but, to my surprise and relief, the 87 came out of its steep turn. That was it – I got the gunsight firmly on him as he straightened, my cannon shells smashed home, and he went in to the sea with an enormous splash. We never did work out what that Stuka had been up to, nor why the pilot had allowed himself to run out of darkness.

'On 8 September, using San Antonio strip near Milazzo as an advanced landing ground, we began to cover the Salerno invasion beaches, over 200 miles away. This involved patrols of over four fours. 600 shot down three enemy bombers that first night and then exacted a steady toll thereafter, though Laurie Dixon and I had no further combats. The patrols were, nevertheless, full of interest as we could see the land battle raging not far from the beaches, where after a few days our advance party under Raleigh Hilken were waiting to welcome us to Monte Corvino airfield. They had an uncomfortable time as Tiger tanks made their nightly forays into the Allied lines. Our route to Salerno was splendidly marked by the perpetual beacon of

Below: **600 Squadron's repair workshop at Cassibile, 1943.**

Left: Beaufighter A-Apple of 600 Squadron, usually flown by the unit commander Wg Cdr Green, and displaying ten victory symbols./*IWM*

Below: Beaufighter RP attacks on enemy shipping were usually highly profitable. Here the 2300-tons *Sabina* comes under rocket onslaught from a 252 Squadron aircraft on 1 June 1944./*V. Cashmore*

Left: **600 Squadron's safety equipment tradesmen check over a Beau's survival dinghy and its accessories.**

Below left: **A 600 Squadron engine mechanic handing a 'precision hammer' to his 'oppo' during a routine engine checkout.**

Stromboli, and as often as not our arrival at the beach-head was greeted with a *feu-de-joie* by the American AA guns. Once again splinters tinkled off the Beau's belly, but I soon learned to take evasive action as soon as I saw muzzle flashes on the ground.

'On 25 September I flew in to Monte Corvino, thereby becoming the first Beaufighter pilot to make a voluntary landing on the mainland of Europe. However, some evil bugs were catching up on me; I flew my last operational sortie with 600 Squadron on September 30, and shortly afterwards succumbed to a two-prong attack by malaria and jaundice. I moved rapidly through Monte Corvino sick quarters – former Italian married quarters – to the Army General Hospital at Salerno. I'm told I was quite ill for a time – I know I had a temperature of over 106-degrees because I sneaked a look at the thermometer – but have no memory of the journey to the hospital. I do, however, have the clearest recollections of a fortnight's convalescence in one of the luxury hotels in Sorrento. What Italian cooks produced from Army rations was nobody's business and, as the staff had just dug up the glorious wines and liqueurs which had been hidden from the Nazis, life was most agreeable. When I recovered I was made tour-expired, having been flying continuously on operations since June 1940, and was home by Christmas.

'I took with me, needless to say, enduring impressions of my nine months with the "Gallant 600". The inspiring leadership of Paddy Green . . . the trust and tolerance of my navigator as fatigue and approaching illness shortened my temper . . . the skill and devotion of the ground crew . . . the high level of experience of the air crews which took a considerable supervisory load off the Flight commanders' backs . . . Warrant Officer Neil, our chief armourer, with his revolver slung low on his hip "High Noon" style . . . James Ritchie, our Canadian radar officer and

gin rummy ace, who flew successful operational sorties as a navigator, though not officially air crew, and won a DFC . . . the skilful and sensitive Doc Scurlock who, unlike me, knew at a glance that the victims of a Marauder crash at Bone who were showing signs of life were past his help, and that those apparently dead would survive . . . the NCO crew which survived a night crash-landing in a forest near Cassibile with just cuts and a badly sprained ankle between them . . . our tame Czech pilot, Joe Hanus, who wept with frustration when he obtained a visual on a Ju88 in the moonlight but couldn't catch it . . . the mystery of the "phantom light" which we and 73 Squadron (Hurricanes) encountered on the enemy side of the lines, looking like a red-hot exhaust but producing no echo on radar AI or GCI . . . and most of all the 100-plus enemy aircraft destroyed in a year for the loss of just one pilot and two navigators killed.'

Eyes in the sky

The value of aerial reconnaissance had its roots in the opening months of the 1914-18 air war, and during World War 2 became a continuing, vital pre-requisite to all land, sea and air operations throughout the war. In the various desert campaigns in North Africa, and later during the Allied advance through Sicily and Italy, such photographic intelligence came to be regarded by army commanders as mandatory prior to launching any land assault; one of its most notable devotees being General Bernard Montgomery. One of the early units to undertake photo-reconnaissance as its prime role was 60 Squadron, SAAF, which throughout 1942 and part of 1943 was commanded by Major O. Glyn Davies (later, Lt-Colonel, DFC):

'At the time I took over command of 60 Squadron in early 1942 it was based at Sidi Barrani in the western desert, equipped with Marylands, then Baltimores, and eventually DH Mosquitos. Initially, the type of operations we were flying were mostly mapping, a role not very popular with the squadron. In order to obtain proper photographs for map-making one has to fly at a constant heading, height and speed, which becomes very boring even in peacetime, though in wartime there was the added

interest of possible interception by enemy fighters, which did happen on a few occasions. But, generally speaking, from Cairo right up to Benghazi operations were fairly trouble-free. It was only when we got into more sensitive areas round El Agheila and, later, Wadi Zem Zem and the Mareth Line that the Germans became distinctly hostile, and it then became obvious that our Marylands and Baltimores were going to be extremely vulnerable.

'The Maryland was a delightful aircraft though somewhat cramped in the cockpit, and with electric constant speed airscrews which gave trouble and were not as reliable as the Hamilton hydraulic type. Our first aircraft were originally destined for the French and were diverted to us after the fall of France. There were some strange signs in the cockpit, for example, *Aterissage* for undercarriage, and *Volettes* for flaps. I believe their throttles originally opened backwards, but (thank Heaven) this had been reversed before we got them. Auxiliary tanks fitted in the bomb bays gave the aircraft an enormous range; on one occasion when my navigator omitted a small matter of 24-degrees westerly variation, I flew for ten hours and fifteen minutes before finding base! So Pratt and Whitney's

Below: **Glyn Davies in the 'office' of a 60 Squadron SAAF Martin Maryland.**/*O. G. Davies*

Top: **Martin Maryland of 60 Squadron SAAF.**/*O. G. Davies*

Above: **Setting out – a DAF Maryland taxying across typical scrub prior to take-off.**

recommendations for economical flight – 1700-1800 rpm and 30-inches boost – really did work . . .

'The Baltimores were not a patch on the Marylands, being heavy and clumsy; though more powerful. They had Wright engines which gave much trouble and couldn't stand up to desert conditions like the Pratt and Whitneys of the Marylands. They were quite heavily armed, including having four fixed guns in the rear compartment, firing under the tail. Probably in a formation they could give quite an account of themselves, but on our lonely flights they were very vulnerable to Messerschmitt Bf109s.

'We were operating directly under the Survey Department of Montgomery's 8th

Army HQ, who became a little touchy when we failed to provide the photographs required; Montgomery was an avid aerial photography fan, and would never launch an attack without extremely good coverage of the target area for both land and artillery operations. When he found we were unable to get him his photographs of certain areas, a degree of ill-will crept in. We kept on trying, and Montgomery's HQ sent an officer down to our unit every morning to sit around and see if any aircraft came back with satisfactory photos. He was very pleasant, a Captain Thompson, who was an expert on wines, but knew very little about aeroplanes. One of our pilots, John Leal, who was photographing the Wadi Zem Zem, was attacked by enemy fighters, had one

Above: **Baltimores of 60 Squadron SAAF over a bald desert landscape in tight formation. Nearest is AG718.**/*O. G. Davies*

engine shot out, suffered further damage when he continued his sortie, and on return to Marble Arch – our base at the time – found the whole area blanked out by a raging sandstorm. With no hydraulics and only one motor, Leal went to the edge of the storm and belly-landed in the desert, fortunately without damage to the camera. We sent out a crew, retrieved the films and processed them, by which time Captain Thompson had taken up his daily station in the Mess and asked if we'd managed to get anything. I explained how Leal had come back and said that he had belly-landed in the desert. "Really?" said Thompson. "With what object in view?" . . .

'However, we still weren't getting the photographs that General Montgomery required and the atmosphere became very strained. I explained to him that it was almost impossible to get the photographic coverage he wanted without more modern, suitable aircraft. "What aircraft do you want then?", he asked. "If we have Mosquitos we should be able to bring in everything you require". He sent a signal asking for us to be equipped with Mosquitos – it was refused. "Any other suggestions?" he then asked. "If we could borrow a Flying Fortress? . . .". He signalled General Eisenhower – again, refused. At that point "Monty" became impatient. Calling one of his staff officers, he ordered, "Send a signal marked personal to Churchill from Montgomery. Unless 60 Squadron, SAAF is equipped with Mosquitos immediately I cannot attack the Mareth Line". Within 24 hours news came through that two Mosquitos would soon be arriving! Then the wonderful news that two Mosquitos were awaiting collection by 60 Squadron, at the Kasfareet Maintenance Unit in the Canal Zone.

'I hastily called up the next pilot on the roster, Oliver Martin, and the two of us took off for Kasfareet immediately. We'd never even seen a Mosquito and didn't really know what to expect, but on arrival there were delighted by the sight of those beautiful aircraft. The only thing that bothered me was that they were the fighter type, and I wondered why on earth the RAF had thought of sending us fighter models with four cannons and four machine guns and no position in the nose for a navigator. It was some time much later that I learned that this pair were coming to Egypt anyway – to be pegged out for testing under tropical temperatures etc!★ However, a Mosquito is a Mosquito!

'The squadron leader in charge of the MU said his instructions were not to allow us to touch the Mosquitos until we'd been "fully briefed" by the delivery pilots, but the latter were "missing" in Cairo, so I persuaded him to give me a short rundown on start-up procedure on Rolls-Royce Merlins – most of my experience had been on radial, air-cooled motors. I then had him have one Mosquito prepared for flight, Martin got into the navigator's seat, I opened up and started down the 1700-yards of PSP serving as a runway. We became airborne, I selected undercarriage "Up" – then Martin asked, "Sir, shouldn't a Mosquito climb at more than 64 knots?" . . . the speed shown at the very bottom of the scale on the ASI! It later transpired that the crew had not removed the cover on the pilot head, high up on the fin! So there I was in a plane I'd never flown before, without any air speed indication. However, we took her up to

★ These were DD743 and DD744; the latter eventually making 60 Sqn's first Mosquito recce sortie on 15 February 1943.

Above: **DH Mosquito MM366, a PR XVI, used by 60 Squadron SAAF.**/*O. G. Davies*

Below right: **Major (later, Lt-Col, DFC) O. G. Davies SAAF in front of a 60 Squadron SAAF Mosquito.**/*O. G. Davies*

height, played around a bit getting the feel, trying out stalling speeds etc, then I brought her in. Fortunately, as I said, there were 1700 yards of runway, most of which were used up in my landing at more than 100 knots . . .

'I then gave Martin an opportunity of flying the Mosquito, and next discussed with the squadron leader how on earth we were going to modify the aircraft for photography. Obviously, we'd need to cut holes in the belly, but as the structure was strange to both of us, this would take time. We finally decided to put a camera under the navigator's seat, and to install a fairly long drift sight through the floor in front of the nav's seat, so that by bending forward he could get his eye to the drift sight and do a run-up to a target. The MU did a jolly good job, but we were stuck there for a week before the modifications were completed. Finally, we left for Castel Benito, whither the squadron had moved during our absence. It was a lovely flight up – at low level, of course, because nobody went high over those areas – and on reaching Castel Benito I did my approach, selected undercarriage "Down", then found to my horror that although both main wheels were down, the tail wheel was not. Telling Martin to go ahead and land, I circuited trying various expedients to get that tail wheel down, but nothing happened. Then the group captain came on the air, "Davies, you are to land immediately – the Prime Minister *(Churchill)* is waiting to meet you!" Obeying this definite order, I came in, gave a sudden hard tug on the stick, and the third green light went on! On being introduced to the great man, he remarked, "You know, Major, I thought there was going to be an accident there". I replied, "Well, that makes two of us!" . . .

'From then on we had enormous success with our Mosquitos. We were able to get General Montgomery all the photographs he wanted, and so successful were these, despite being from clumsily-converted aircraft installations, that some of the photographs were reported by the map-makers as being the first pictures they'd received equal in quality to peacetime work. We were rather proud of that, and at the end of Montgomery's campaign he paid a very handsome tribute in his order of the day, when he said that the success of his campaign in North Africa had been largely due to the "magnificent air photography" with which he had been provided.

'We were greatly interested in strategic

reconnaissance photography, though in North Africa there was very little of that to do. It was only towards the end of my first tour of operations when one of the proudest moments I had as commander of 60 Squadron occurred. My Operations Officer, Captain Hunter, and I were ordered to Cairo to report to some form of special HQ. We flew down, were duly picked up, taken to an area I didn't know, and threaded through three lines of barbed wire with tremendous security "screening" and flashing of passes etc. Inside we were taken among a lot of top brass who were planning the Sicily invasion, told directly of the intention to invade, and asked to provide complete photographic coverage of the whole of Sicily. This was an operation which turned out to be easier than anticipated due to the magnificent co-operation of Malta's radar. It was possible to go out in the Mosquito and sit back and concentrate entirely on the mapping, until Malta radio called up and said, "Thirteen unpleasant gentlemen approaching – suggest you go home." Then we'd break off and buzz off – back again that afternoon or next day and able to do a couple of hours' flying normally under Malta's watchful eye; so the whole operation went off extremely well.

'When the North African campaign ended we did one or two operations over Europe from North Africa, but then the squadron moved entirely to San Severo in central Italy. There we were firmly established as a unit of the American 90th Wing Reconnaissance, under the command of Colonel Carl G.

Prolifca, Jr, with a Wg Cdr Fuller as his second-in-command. It was a period when we were short of aircraft; we had spare pilots but no aircraft for them to fly – a most demoralising situation. It meant too bad luck for the pilots as they took much longer to finish their operational tours. One American squadron there was flying Lockheed P-38 F-5s – photographic Lightnings – and had more aircraft than pilots, so I came to a very happy arrangement that while we were short of aircraft perhaps we could operate in Lightnings. They agreed and for quite a while this worked most satisfactorily. I did only one operation in a Lightning and wasn't very happy. I missed my navigator and, frankly, didn't think the Lightning could compare with the Mosquito. At altitude – we normally operated our Mosquitos at about 32-35,000 feet – the Lightning didn't appear to have the performance of a Mossie. It was a very heavy plane, and incorporated some strange American ideas in it, such as a handle rather like a saloon car for winding the cockpit window up and down. However, it was better than nothing. In time we were fully equipped with Mosquitos and, with grateful thanks, were able to hand back to the Americans their Lightnings.

'We ranged very far in those days, right up to the Black Sea and Warsaw and then back, picking up places like Augsburg and Regensburg on the way back to photograph their submarine engine works and Messerschmitt factories respectively. When one got

Below: **60 Squadron SAAF's most famous Mosquito, *Lovely Lady,* a PR IX, undergoing servicing at San Severo.**/*O. G. Davies*

Top: **Spitfire flown on PR sorties from the Suez Canal zone.**/*V. Cashmore via D. Vincent*

Above: **Spitfire IX modified for PR work with the SAAF.**/*via T. Hooton*

back from five or six hours' flying – lone and intense flights – it should be remembered that we were flying completely unpressurised planes, and six hours up to 32,000 feet was a bit telling on the constitution. We subsequently got pressurised Mosquitos – Mk XVIs I believe – but they were completely useless; no matter what we did we couldn't get rid of the fogging up of the windscreen. At one stage I asked my engineering officer to open up the sandwich windscreen which was fitted with a little tube leading to a silica gel container to withdraw moisture. I asked him to put silica gell cyrstals right inside the windscreen. When "Bette" Davis [Lt J. Elwyn 'Bette' Davis, later Captain, OBE] and I set off to test this out we flew through some electrical disturbances and the silica gel crystals promptly sprang up and coated themselves firmly all over the inside of the windscreen, completely blocking vision out front. Fortunately, there was a tiny little bad vision window on the left-hand side and I had to open this and almost put my eye to it in order to come in and land at our base at San Severo.

'We greatly enjoyed the long strategic reconnaissance flights over Germany. We would be called into Captain Hunter's office which had a huge wall map, a thing about 15 by 20 feet, covered with dozens of little coloured flags; each with different colours representing periods at which these targets had to be photographed. A green flag meant coverage every fortnight, others meant weekly, and finally we got down to every three days. This sort of photography intrigued us, and we went over Ploesti very often to do the pre-bombing photographs and subsequent bomb damage assessment pictures. Ploesti became slightly dangerous when the Americans started operating there with hordes of Liberators and things, because they used to take along about 500 Mustangs as escort. Sometimes there was a slight difference in timings – the Americans would arrive early or perhaps we would arrive later over the target – and it was quite terrifying to see about 500 Mustangs bearing down on one poor little Mosquito!

'Normally if we saw Messerschmitt Bf109s or Focke Wulf Fw 190s in time we could get away quite easily – just jettison our wing tanks, open up, and beat it, either for the next target on the list or hang around a bit and return after the fighters had disappeared.

Above: **Spitfire PR IV modified by 103 MU, Aboukir. It was later used by 680 Squadron in 1943 for sorties over Salonika. The patchwork quilt appearance resulted from being rubbed down at Aboukir for smoother surfaces, hence marginally greater speed etc./Wg Cdr T. Cooper-Slipper**

When those fighters were on our tail that little bit of armour plate behind my back seemed to get very, very narrow! In my own case I had a fairly lucky time in this respect, and my most dangerous experiences were the several occasions when the Americans very nearly shot me down! They had a curious outlook on this, assuring me solemnly that a Mosquito looked exactly like a Ju 88 – which I found hard to believe. For just one example, "Bette" Davis and I were flying back from the South of France on one occasion and were going past the northern tip of Corsica when "Bette" said, "Two Focke Wulfs coming up astern". I prepared to jettison tanks and make off, saying "Are you sure?". He then said, "No, no, hang on, they're jinking a bit and I can see they're American Thunderbolts". "You're quite sure?" . . . "Yes, I can see the stars on their fuselages when they weave". So I relaxed and sat back – then things started to fly off the Mosquito and I had to jettison the tanks and make for home smartly!

'Next night I was in our very popular Allied Officers' Club in the opera house at San Severo and as I walked in was greeted by several American lieutenants who offered me a drink. We got chatting about what "ships" I flew and when I said Mosquitos, they said "Aw, we fly P-47s, stationed in Corsica. Yesterday we saw a ship which we saw was a Ju88, so we chased it. When we got up near we recognised it was a Mosquito, but were so pissed off that we shot at it anyway!" When I suggested they might be interested to know that that was me, they said, "Waal, have another drink, Major". At that moment another American pilot came in whom they introduced as their Flight commander – "First Lootenant Brown. He's got nine victories confirmed – four of them friendly!" . . . I was finally forced to go to General Spaatz to complain about the harassment we were receiving from American fighters. He didn't seem deeply concerned. "These boys have to be on the alert and I don't mind if they're a bit trigger-happy!" He then suggested that we paint broad white bands around the mainplanes and fuselage because he understood that this was what they intended doing with the planes they were going to use in the invasion of France. We did that and I flew one right around all the American fighter aerodromes to demonstrate these markings – but we continued to have incidents when they gave us a hard time.

'We very much enjoyed in Italy the arrival of Mosquitos from Benson in the UK, from where they had taken off early in the morning and come right across Europe, landed in San Severo, and had the films removed from their cameras – and sometimes had these processed by us. Then, with cameras reloaded, in due course they flew off back to England. Why we particularly enjoyed these visitors was because they used to bring us that morning's London newspapers. We took great delight in spreading these papers round on the table in our mess tent, then inviting up some of the anti-aircraft "bow and arrow" boys for a drink. We watched them pick up a London paper, look at the date, glance uneasily around, then shuffle the paper back onto the table as if they'd been caught out in something rather disgraceful! It was quite a long time before they realised that these papers were quite genuine, and that we regularly – sometimes two or three times a week – had the London papers of that particular morning.

'From my point of view, I felt myself extremely lucky and very proud to have had command of 60 Squadron. It was a small squadron, a specialist squadron, and we seemed to have the really magnificent types. The two adjutants who served under me, Captain Young and, subsequently, Captain Stevenson, couldn't have been better fellows, and relieved their CO entirely of any administrative work, and did everything that was required. We had a marvellous operations officer, Captain Hunter; an excellent engineering officer Captain Sharman; and generally speaking the squadron was made up of the greatest bunch of fellows I've known. I always remember 60 Squadron as a very happy squadron.'

Kiwi fighter

Evan Mackie – 'Rosie' to his intimates – hailed from Otorohanga, New Zealand and joined the RNZAF in 1941. Coming to England the following year as a fighter pilot, Mackie eventually ended the war with a DSO, DFC and Bar and a credited victory tally in excess of 20. His part in the desert war commenced late in 1942 when he arrived as one of 243 Squadron's pilots:

'Operating from makeshift airstrips and living under canvas in Tunisia came as a bit of a shock after the comparative comforts of the permanent RAF stations in the UK, but the good flying conditions and the fact that we saw lots of action in this new theatre of war was ample compensation. One could not but think that we were really making a contribution to the war effort. In this campaign we carried out high-level sweeps and medium bomber escorts, but our main task, and that which resulted in most action with enemy aircraft, was that of patrolling the front line area – or "bomb line", as it was usually called. The performance of the Spitfire Vb was comparable with that of the aircraft we encountered, and I'm sure that the damage which we inflicted far exceeded the losses we sustained.

'At the conclusion of this campaign we moved to Malta and continued to harass the retreating enemy into Sicily – medium and heavy bomber escorts being the order of the day. The cool buildings and abundance of fresh water on Malta provided a welcome change from the heat and flies of Tunisia. At this stage the camouflage of our aircraft was changed to dark green colours in keeping with the Sicilian and Italian countrysides. We encountered enemy aircraft on the majority of sorties, including many Italians, but these were never much of a threat and seldom stayed long enough to engage in combat. On one particular occasion my section of four got split up at 26,000 feet over Catania, Sicily, and I found myself alone in a clear blue sky with no less than six Messerschmitt Bf 109s who seemed hell-bent on my destruction. I was getting nowhere fast and was a long way from home, so decided that my only hope of salvation was to out-dive my opponents despite their acknowledged superiority in this manoeuvre. I claim to be pretty ham-fisted when it comes to driving aeroplanes – which is probably the reason for my survival – but only careful manipulation of the trim tabs got me out of that dive all in one piece, and as I flattened out over the sea at zero feet a line of bullets splashed into the glassy surface of the water just to one side of me. I didn't sight my adversary but obviously he'd followed me down, taken a pot-shot, and departed before I could execute a turn.

'I was on the first patrol which covered the invasion of Sicily on 10 July 1943, and four days later we moved to a hastily constructed landing strip on the beach-head – again under canvas. Operations once more comprised army support, bomber escorts, etc until the

Below: **Squadron Leader E. D. Mackie DSO, DFC when OC 92 Sqn in Italy in 1943-44.**/*IWM*

Below right: **E. D. Mackie and 92 Squadron, Italy. Mackie is fifth from left standing, while second from left, standing, is F. J. Edwards.**/*E. D. Mackie*

98

Germans retreated to Italy. We had several moves in Sicily but finally established ourselves at a strip called Cassala, on the north coast of the island. Then on 9 September 1943 it was announced that the Italians had capitulated, and at dawn that day Allied forces made their historic landings at Salerno. Air cover was provided by the Spitfires based at Cassala and once again I was one of the first on the scene. Salerno was 170 miles across the ocean from Cassala, so that even with 90-gallons long-range tanks fitted we could not spend more than 30 minutes or so on actual patrol without jeopardising our chances of getting back to base. Operating Spitfires at this range, especially across the water, was unheard of at that time, but thanks to the high standard of our aircraft maintenance we were able to provide cover at squadron strength, twice daily, for five days without mishap.

'On 13 September the landing forces had established a precarious toe-hold at Salerno, sufficient for our move to an airstrip only a stone's throw from the beach and perilously near to the German lines. So close in fact that our artillery was firing across the air strip, and our "circuit" had to be confined to the seaward side to avoid German rifle fire. Operations consisted mainly of patrols over the "bomb line", but we encountered few enemy aircraft. At this stage the weather began to deteriorate somewhat and torrential rain and tornadoes caused some anxious moments. The ground forces gradually expanded their perimeter until they became bogged down at the Volturno River, and in the ensuing stalemate we moved to Capodichino near Naples.

'My appointment as commanding officer of 92 Squadron, then based on the east coast of Italy, came on 5 November. As this was – then – the top-scoring fighter squadron in the RAF, I regarded this as something of an honour. They were flying Spitfire VIIIs, which were definitely superior to any of the enemy aircraft we encountered in Italy, especially above 15,000 feet. Operations in this area were mainly patrols over the Sangro River area, and there was considerable enemy aircraft activity. Although it was almost mid-winter we were still under canvas, but morale was always good and there were never any complaints. However, we did notice that the cold was intense as we gained altitude, and extra gloves made little difference. The ground forces once again bogged down at the Sangro River, probably because of the atrocious weather conditions, and on 17 January 1944 we moved back near Naples to augment fighter cover available for the forthcoming landings at Anzio, near Rome. Yet again I was to witness the spectacle of large-scale landings at dawn on 22 January, and was beginning to regard myself as something of a specialist in this field – I'd also covered the Dieppe raid back in August 1942!

'Opposition from enemy aircraft was slow to develop and it was not until 16 February that

Below left: **'Imshi' Mason (centre) and P. H. Dunn (rt), 274 Squadron.**/*Mrs J. Strange via C. Laubscher*

Below: **Squadron Leader P. H. Dunn, OC 274 Sqn and a unit Hurricane.**/*Mrs J. Strange via C. Laubscher*

Bottom: **To pilots used to the domestic clutter of an English aerodrome, desert landing grounds came as something of a shock – naked sand or scrub bereft of buildings. Here Hurricanes of 94 Squadron get airborne from LG 109 in 1941.**/*M. Gidman*

92 Squadron reached its long-awaited target of 300 enemy aircraft destroyed. There were several instances of engine failure with our Spitfire VIIIs whilst travelling to or from patrol, and it was ultimately discovered that this was due to petrol *freezing up* in a small wing radiator between the main tanks and the carburettor. In normal temperatures this radiator prevented petrol from 'boiling' at the reduced atmospheric pressure after a fast climb which the aircraft was capable of, but in the Italian winter climate it was unnecessary – a patch over the radiator cured the problem.

'At the end of February 1944 I was posted "operational tour-expired," having completed 492 ops' hours and 349 sorties for my first tour, and returned to England for a six-months' stint at HQ, Air Defence of Great Britain before resuming operations with 2nd TAF (Tactical Air Force) at Volkel in Holland on Hawker Tempests until the end of hostilities in Europe.'

Fragments

Life in the Desert Air Force, at any period of its existence, offered a myriad of varying experiences, physical, mental and spiritual. Almost any man claiming proud membership of that gallant company could probably fill a book with his individual tale. Thus even to attempt to illustrate every facet of life among those desert warriors would be an impossible goal. Nevertheless, perhaps the following brief glimpses into the feelings, experiences, humour *et al* of a random cross-section of DAF men can at least give something of the flavour of the airmen's reactions to their nomadic existence under the ever-hovering sun of Mediterranean backdrop. For most men their time with the DAF was a unique period in their lives; meeting peoples and seeing places only read about in geography books at school previously, living in primitive conditions bereft of all things except the barest necessities to sustain life and enable them to do the job. In the desert in particular they found themselves in almost daily combat with a land naturally hostile to prolonged human existence, in circumstances where raw nature was as great, if not far greater an implacable foe than any human opponent. Perversely, surviving in such conditions bred a comradeship and brotherhood which had few equals, and engendered a fierce, deep loyalty among all ranks – a cohesive spirit which was the very base rock foundation of the DAF's ultimate triumph.

Christmas 1940 saw 274 Squadron based at Sidi Haneish, just inland from Egypt's Mediterranean coastline, about 150-odd miles west of Alexandria:
'Sidi Haneish lay at the top of an escarpment and was exposed to every wind that blew. From this 'drome "Imshi" Mason, "Nobby" Clark and "Judy" Garland made daily sorties against the Italians. Taking off at dawn, the formations of Hurricanes roared away, leaving a trail of black exhaust fumes in the cold winter air. The ground crews eagerly awaited their return, and there were smiles of satisfaction on the faces of those crews who recognised their returning pilots doing a victory roll over the 'drome, thus notifying the squadron of their success. Not a day passed

Left: **The desert wasn't all golden sand and sunshine . . . a bomber crew bale out their 'bivvy' in Tunisia.**

Above: **Sqn Ldr E. M. Mason DFC – 'Imshi' – who served with Nos 45, 80, 274, 261 and 260 Sqns before his death in action over Martuba airfield on 15 February 1942. Seen here in his 80 Sqn-badged white flying overall, and sporting his famous beard.**

but the jubilant pilots gave vent to their satisfaction at besting the Axis by shooting up the 'drome and doing victory rolls. To this 'drome many pilots limped home with the fuselage of their kites riddled with bullet holes, but they gave far more than they ever received.

'A great amount of captured war material found its way from the forward areas to the 'drome. Motor-cycles, staff cars, transport of every description including push-bikes, were soon in evidence. Flight Sergeants would go their rounds in Italian staff cars, whilst the commanding officer, "Paddy" Dunn, could be seen calling at the Orderly Room riding a brand-new motor-bike. Soon all ranks from the lowest erk upwards had obtained some form of enemy transport to propel them over the bumpy desert scrub that surrounded the 'drome. Ground crews who walked from kite to kite doing their various jobs were looked upon as having their fingers in. Foraging parties returned with rifles, ammunition, Breda guns and all the paraphernalia of war that the fleeing Italians had left behind.

'The big event, however, was to be Christmas. The men were rather disappointed at not being able to spend their Christmas near the fleshpots of Alexandria, but this disappointment quickly vanished when they were confronted with the amazing Christmas spread laid before them by the squadron cooks. Christmas in the western desert at Sidi Haneish was the first that many of the men had spent away from their homes, and they were determined to do all in their power to capture the festive spirit. Parties sprang into being in every tent, as the occupants armed with beer and other luxuries commenced activities. By nightfall all was as merry as the proverbial marriage belle.

'On Christmas Day, those who were capable of doing so struggled over to breakfast before beginning the day's fun and games. Christmas Day in the Services is the day when strict discipline is relaxed. A day when the stiffest officer unbends and mumbles "A Merry Christmas, lads". A day on which erks have been known to call the officers "Snow" and "Chum" – and get away with it. After the dinner, which had all the things necessary to warrant it being called "wizard", the CO spoke a few words to the officers and men. Then the fun commenced. Soon the air was vibrant to the crack of Italian rifles as the boys indulged in a little target practice. The pilots, most of them having obtained Italian motor-cycles, indulged in a little fancy track racing across the 'drome, and tried their skill at broadsiding. At night, a high tea completed the day's menu.'

'Imshi', mentioned in the foregoing account, referred to Flying Officer Ernest Mitchelson Mason, a pre-war RAF officer who was eventually to rise to Squadron Leader, DFC before his death in action, credited with a tally of at least 17 victories in aerial combat. A prolific letter-writer to his mother in England, Mason wrote the following on 23 December 1940:

'Immediately I arrived back after my night in Alex [Alexandria] I found your congratulatory telegram awaiting me [referring to his recent promotion to Flying Officer]. Very good news. My one night in Alex was very pleasant as although we have only been here a couple of weeks I was in need of a bath.

'The morning after I got back I went on patrol early in the morning and got two S.79s [Italian Savoia-Marchetti bombers]. The first one was well over Italian territory and was all alone making for home and only just off the ground. I got behind him and gave him a short burst. His port engine caught fire and he managed to get his aircraft down with wheels up. I didn't bother to fire again but flew alongside and watched as I hadn't seen one crash close to yet. However, he bounced twice and slid on his belly and tipped on his nose. Out of the crew of five or six only one got out [one of the two pilots]. He stood looking at the wrecked machine so miserably that I hadn't the heart to machine-gun him.

'After this I climbed up and after a bit I saw a large formation below me of ten S.79s and about 20 fighters. I dived past the escort and shot at one of the outside bombers and dived away. After climbing again I saw that although this chap had dropped back at first, he had not got back in formation. I hung around above for about ten minutes and then whilst they were dropping their bombs I chose my opportunity and dived very steeply on this same fellow. As the escorting fighters saw me

Above: **Savoia SM79s of the Italian 10 Squadriglia – common foes for 80 Sqn's Gladiators in 1940.**

coming in plenty of time I had to continue my dive and away, closely pursued by extremely angry CR 42s. So I did not observe the result of my engagement, though I saw my bullets going into him. I was not going to claim this one. However, another pilot saw an S.79 burning on the bround near this encounter so I have been told that I can have this as confirmed. Also, a later report from the Army states that it was seen going down in flames. So that made two S.79s for one morning!

'In lieu of some other crest or device I have put the Blackpool coat of arms on my machine. The mess corporal, who also comes from Blackpool and is a bit of an artist, has done it beautifully on a large aluminium shield which is bolted to the side of the fuselage. So far, all my five confirmed victories are with this crest. The unconfirmed one was with another machine, not my own.

'I find I have a bullet hole in one of the petrol tanks, presumably as a result of this morning's show. Although I did not notice anything, I must have had quite a concentration of crossfire from the bomber formation as well as return fire from the rear gunner of the first lone aircraft. This is the first bullet hole I have had! I consider that one should inflict as much damage with as little damage to oneself as possible. To attack the large formation on my own *once* was good surprise tactics; but the second time was bad tactics because the element of surprise was lacking. Of course, I was safe enough because of the speed I developed in my dive, but the chance of getting anything down was equally small. It was only luck that I got the bomber.

'I am very comfortable in a bell tent. I have my camp bed – I have used it for two years so am quite used to it – and a decent-sized table I had made some time ago, and two chairs. I

have an oil lamp and a Valor heater. We have a wooden mess which is quite comfortable. I like it here very much because I can stop in my flying gear all day until bedtime which more than compensates for lack of other facilities. I wear shorts, shirt and flying boots with that white sweater and my white overalls. In this, and my beard, I am really happy and comfortable. I have the Fiat and the motor-cycle parked outside my tent.'

On 15 February 1942, as a newly-promoted Squadron Leader and latest commander of 94 Squadron, Mason led a strafing sortie against Martuba airfield, but was killed over the target by Oberfeldwebel Schulz of II/JG 27, who claimed four other victories in this same combat.

Clive Caldwell hailed from Sydney, Australia, learned to fly privately, then joined the RAAF in September 1939. In early 1941 he joined 250 Squadron in the desert, flying Tomahawks, and scored his first confirmed combat victory on 26 June 1941. His cool determination, aggressiveness, and skill soon earned him the nickname of 'Killer', and in January 1942 he became commander of 112 'Shark' Squadron. By the end of the war he had been awarded DSO, DFC and was credited with at least 27 victories. One of Caldwell's high-scoring sorties was on 5 December 1941, while still serving with 250 Squadron:

'I was leading the formation of two squadrons, 112 acting as top cover to 250 Squadron to patrol a line approximately ten miles west of El Gubi and had just reached this position at 1140 hours when I received R/T warning that a large enemy formation was approaching from the north-west at our height. Both squadrons climbed immediately and within a

minute the enemy formation consisting of Ju87s with fighter escort was sighted on our starboard side. 250 Squadron went into line-astern behind me and as 112 engaged the escorting fighters, we attacked the Ju87s from the rear quarter. At 300 yards I opened fire with all my guns at the leader of one of the rear sections of three, allowing too little deflection, and hit No 2 and No 3, one of which burst into flames immediately, the other going down smoking and went into flames after losing about 1000 feet. I then attacked the leader of the rear section from below and behind, opening fire with all guns at very close range. The enemy aircraft turned over and dived steeply down with the root of the starboard wing in flames. At another Stuka I opened fire again at close range, the enemy caught fire and crashed in flames near some dispersed mechanised transport. I was then able to pull up under the belly of the one at the rear, holding the burst until very close range. The enemy aircraft diced gently straight ahead streaming smoke, caught fire, then dived into the ground.'

One of the 'founder-members' of the DAF was 112 Squadron, RAF, a unit which had been stationed in the Middle East since May 1939, at which time it had been equipped with Gladiators. In the next two years it fought through virtually every campaign, including Greece and Crete, and by early 1942 was based at El Adem, flying Kittyhawks under the command of Sqn Ldr Clive Caldwell. In September 1941, the squadron had been equipped with Tomahawks, and in that month came the first appearance of a squadron marking which was to be associated with 112 thereafter – the famous 'Shark's Teeth' insigne. The Tomahawk, and later Kitty-

hawk, lent themselves admirably to such a marking, with their large pointed spinners and under-nose gaping intakes; and to many people even today the 'Sharksmouth' automatically recalls the Desert Air Force. 112 Squadron was to fight throughout the Middle East war, without let-up until the final victory in Italy in 1945. As merely one example of the 'Sharks' prowess, a large dogfight on 14 February 1942 resulted in one of the squadron's most successful days in action; as recorded in the squadron history★ (*History of 112 Squadron 1917-57* by Flt Lt R. A. Brown; 1959):

'On the 14th there was another of the fine squadron victories that had been absent from the squadron for so long. Ten Kittyhawks led by Plt Off Bartle in AK700, with Sgt Simonsen (AK682), Plt Off N. Duke (AK578), Sgt Leu (AK781), Plt Off Dickenson (AK804), Sgt Evans (AK637), Sgt Drew (AK653), Sgt Christie (AK761), Sgt Cordwell (AK630), Sgt Burney (AK702), and eight aircraft from No 3 RAAF Squadron, were scrambled to meet an approaching enemy formation. After flying north to Tobruk the Kittyhawks turned west over the perimeter defences and climbed steadily until, over Acroma, 3 Sqn were flying at 8000ft with 112 slightly ahead and above, just below the cloud base, and at an ideal height for the Kittyhawk.

'At this moment they spotted about a dozen Macchi 200s and 202s in a loose Vic-formation about 2000ft below, to the left and in front. Plt Off Bartle warned the Australians, who had, however, already seen a formation of enemy bombers with close cover escort, flying at less than 2000 feet. 112 concentrated on the fighters who by now were climbing to meet the attack. Their courage failed them and they hurriedly tried to form a defensive circle, in a half-hearted fashion. The Kittyhawks dived into them and in the initial attack every aircraft of 112 Squadron must have hit something. Sgt Burney, having dived through the formation, saw the bombers below, they were BR65s, and so he carried on and shot one down. This aircraft attempted to evade but it hit the ground, and Burney "strafed him to save him a walk home . . ." By the time he regained the formation there were no enemy fighters to be seen amongst the milling Kittyhawks. Sgt Cordwell, in his first action, shot away about three-quarters of the wing of an Me109F which spun in out of control. Sgt Evans attacked a M.200 as it was turning and shot about two feet off its starboard wing. It dived steeply and was probably destroyed. Sgt Drew, also on his first real engagement, got himself two M.200s, one of which he saw hit the ground – "It was as easy as breakfast in bed", he is recorded as saying.

'Plt Off Duke attacked an M.200 which was seen to spin in and crash by Sgt Evans. He also

attacked another Macchi at ground level from dead astern and it flew into the ground and burst into flames. This kill was shared with Sgt Reid of 3 RAAF who was in *(Kittyhawk)* CV-W. The enemy's defence was to adopt a circle, and when evading, to dive down to ground level in rolls and vertical dives. Sgt Leu attacked an M.200 which blew up, and another one which went into the ground. Sgt Simonsen certainly destroyed an M.200 which he saw spin into the ground, and probably damaged another. Plt Off Dickenson made a stern attack on another M.200 which was then enveloped in a sheet of flame at 1000 feet. Sgt Christie claimed two M.200s destroyed and one damaged. His account was that he dived and gave one Macchi a heavy burst so that the aircraft climbed steeply, then spiralled down and crashed, bursting into flames. He dived on the second, which stalled, pouring out black smoke and going into a dive. He had a go at a third and probably damaged it but without any visible result. Sgt Evans also attacked an M.200 which dived away so steeply that it is doubtful whether it could have pulled out. Plt Off Bartle gave another M.200 a good burst which sent it down out of control, and damaged a Bf109F which he chased all the way to Tmimi.

'No 3 Squadron, in the meanwhile, were about to fall on the bombers when they saw six Bf109Fs lurking about. They wheeled round in time and in the ensuing dogfight four Bf109s were destroyed and another damaged. They then concentrated on the bombers. By the end of the fight the remnants of the enemy formation had fled. Of the estimated total strength at the beginning of 32 enemy aircraft,

20 were claimed as destroyed, two probably destroyed, and ten damaged. Neither of the Kittyhawk squadrons lost an aircraft in what was a text-book example of perfect interception – both top and extra cover being eliminated before the bombers were attacked. No 3 RAAF Squadron were particularly pleased with their success as a lot of their pilots were newcomers. 112 Squadron's share of this total was eleven and a half destroyed, two probables, and three damaged. In the fight 112 had fired 7060 rounds.'

Dogfights and sorties aside, life in the DAF, both in Africa and Italy, had its more mundane aspects; not least the many vicissitudes incumbent with the needs of nature when leading a nomadic existence. Sun, sand, flies, fever, added to a general lack

Below: **AVM Harry Broadhurst talks to squadron and flight commanders of 239 Wing in Sicily, September 1943. Personalities numbered are (1) Broadhurst, (2) Wg Cdr Johnny Darwen DSO, DFC, and (3) Wg Cdr Borg.**/*Dr F. T. Pearce*

of all but the barest necessities, gave DAF men a simple philosophy – as long as the job is done, the rest can wait. One natural phenomenon experienced by all throughout the North African campaigns was the hot desert windstorm – the *khamsin* (pronounced *kam-seen*) against which there was no real protection. Ex-Leading Aircraftman (LAC) Tingle, an armament mechanic with 112 Squadron, describes his experiences:
'112 Squadron was always up with the Army, and therefore our living conditions were what we made them – a dugout in the sand with a bivouac cover over the top. For a bed, a piece of sacking nailed over two lumps of wood, with two end pieces to keep it tight. Of course, not everyone had it so comfy . . . for some it was just their two *(issue)* blankets and head down in the sand! Then there were sand-storms. One could see them coming, a large brown cloud far off in the distance. That was the time to get out a ball of string, tie one end to a stick in your dugout, and take the other end to the "cookhouse". Sometimes these storms lasted three or four days, and to be lost in a sand-storm – well, only those who *have* been lost in one can know what it was like.'

In June 1942, No 417 Squadron RCAF arrived in Egypt, flying Hurricanes, later Spitfires, in defence of the Suez Canal/Delta zones. Then, in April 1943, it joined the DAF, and stayed with it until the end of the war – the DAF's only RCAF squadron. After several weeks of operations in the front line, 417's crews were sent on a toughening-up (sic) course in preparation for the forthcoming invasion of Sicily; a detachment which drew the following comments from the squadron commander, Sqn Ldr F. B. Foster;
'We have lived in the sand under canvas since our arrival in the Middle East, and by this time are quite inured to the heat of the day and the cold of the night, sand, flies, fleas and mosquitoes, endless bully beef and hard tack – all aside from the expected hazards of war with the Eighth Army. Our ground crews are the only Canadian airmen who are real front-line soldiers, exposed to bombing, strafing, and the threat of German commando raids. This has but made them the keenest ground crew in the RCAF, since they have a very personal interest in the efficiency of the fighters overhead.

'Our relaxations are few. Cards and letter-writing fill our evenings, whilst swimming, when we are near the Med, and softball are our recreations. Just as it is possible to follow the route of the New Zealand divisions from Alamein to Agheila by abandoned rugger fields, so our path could be traced by rough baseball diamonds in the sand. No gang of back-lot kids ever treasured

Above: **Spitfire IX, JK887 at Sorman/Zavia, Tripolitania in July 1943 gets an engine check, with necessary pair of erks to keep the tail on the deck.**/*M. Gidman*

two bats and three well-worn balls as do we. Our other exercise is the immediate digging of slit trenches after each of our frequent moves. Each tent takes as much pride in its trench as a householder does in her garden, and they brag about the speed with which they dive into theirs when occasion arises.

'In addition, we have the finest five-piece swing band in the desert, led by Plt Off Johnny Koplitz of Hoboken, former American band-leader, and greatly in demand by Army and Air Force units far and near. Lacking movies and concert parties, this band has filled in many a dull evening. "Toughening up" they say?? . . .

Sometime about June 1941 Squadron Leader George W. Houghton, a press officer, got together with a colleague and formed the 'Late Arrivals Club' – an exclusive company whose only qualification for membership was that air crews had to walk back from behind enemy lines after being brought or shot down. A metal flying boot with wings on the heel was awarded to suitable applicants, and a certificate duly signed, dated and witnessed was issued to each "Late Arrival". The club's motto was simple – It's never too late to come back. Initially, Houghton had 50 badges made by a Cairo metal-beater, but the membership soon passed the hundred mark within the first year of the club's inauguration. Every member's story was different – each a mini-epic of courage and determination, privation and dogged endurance. Though, pedantically speaking, not members of the DAF, the tale of two bomber crew members of 40 Squadron RAF epitomises the men who wore a silver winged boot on their left breast tunic pocket. On the night of 7 October 1942, Flight Sergeant R. Spence, RCAF was skipper of Wellington DV504, 'G', from Kabrit, on a bombing sortie to Tobruk. At about 0300 hours next morning, as he circled Tobruk harbour, flak found one of his engines, set it

on fire, and its propeller flew off. The six-man crew baled out in good order, but only four managed to gather in the darkness subsequently – of the other two they knew nothing. At dawn Spence checked out their survival rations – and chances. As far as they could figure it, they faced some 350 miles of desert to cross if they were to regain friendly territory. Between them they counted four small compasses, three full water bottles, six tins of bully, some chewing gum, chocolate, toffee and milk tablets, and 16 packets of hard tack biscuits. Two of them – both air gunners – had ankle injuries. That day, 8 October, they walked until 1600 hours, stopping only to fill a spare two-gallon tin with water from a cairn they discovered en route. Their subsequent progress was recorded in a diary: '*Second day.* Set course south-east. Found water-hole, had good drink. At mid-day rest and ate a can of bully. 1800 hours made camp by water hole. Six Hindus escaped from Tobruk came up to camp, well provisioned and plenty of water. Gave them compass. Said they were heading south into desert. Sgt B [A. W. Butteriss, Rear AG] was weak, his ankle giving trouble.

'*Fourth Day.* Drank out of tin and ate some milk tablets. Two Ju 88s passed overhead, very close and low, took cover. Sighted barbed wire ahead. 1030 hrs crossed border line south of Sollum. Heat terrific. Sheltered from sun under u/s lorry. B's birthday party, had first good laugh. Sgt B is very weak, Sgt L [E. A. Linforth, AG] also very weak and bad ankle, flying boots making it very hard to walk. Going very hard, loose rocks, unable to get good footholds.

'*Sixth day.* 0830 made camp [having walked all night], sleep almost impossible. 1730 hrs broke camp, ate one can of chocolate, 16 biscuits, milk tablets. Set course due east. 2030 hrs arrived at u/s German lorry with four cans petrol inside, no water. Here Sgt B decided to leave us. He had been through hell

Above: **239 Wing Mustang, duly bombed up with two 1000lb bombs, trundling to take-off point, Italy early 1944./*Dr F. T. Pearce***

since our starting, despite efforts to help and assist him. He was wearing flying boots which gave him very little support walking over loose rocks. At every rest made throughout six days he was with us. He used to fall down on all fours beside our leaky water can and sucked what water seeped out. It was horrible. He was very close to coast, we could see patrolling planes flying east and west all day and were very close to railroad. He gave us his mother's address, also address of his girlfriend. We left him with two bottles of water and one can of chocolate and walked south-east.* We walked all night, hard going.

'*Eighth Day.* By now we figured we are somewhat south of Sidi Barrani. Our next pinpoint will be the Mersa Matruh-Siwa Oasis road. Hope to reach same in two or three nights. 1700 hrs started walking, course slightly south of east. 1800 hrs, here Sgt L decided to leave us. Like Sgt B, he has had a tough time since starting, it was cruel, since leaving Sollum we have been walking on loose rock. Figuring him to be no more than a day/day and a half from coast, we left him a water can with two bottles of water in same, tin of chocolate, a chocolate bar, some milk tablets and some gum. He was very game. He gave us his mother's address, wanted us to notify her of his safety. We left him in shelter of a u/s lorry. [Sgt Linforth was also made a prisoner of war later]. Between the two of us [Flt Sgt Spence and Sgt J. K. Wood, RAAF] we now had left four tins of bully beef, three tins ration chocolate, about 16 biscuits, about

* Sgt Butteries was made a prisoner of war shortly after.

20 milk tablets, three full water bottles, two empty same, our two-gallon tin about three parts full. Having reckoned on trek taking us 20 days at beginning, and having walked eight, we rationed accordingly for remainder. We tried to make a can of bully beef last the two of us three days.

'*Tenth Day.* Started walking course south-east, hard going, rocks and sandstorm. Found old tomb, decided to remain all night, very fatigued, sandstorm intense. Slept all night.

'*Twelfth Day.* Met two Arabs driving camels to Siwa Oasis. They gave us three pints of water and two handfuls of dates for 45 piastres (all money we had). Also gave us good drink and smoke out of a pipe, home-grown tobacco. Smoke floored us.

'*Fourteenth Day.* Had a little rain shower. Managed good drink out of rock pool, not enough to collect. Sole falling off Sgt W's shoe, had to fix. F/Sgt S's boot also in miserable condition.

'*Fifteenth Day.* Shoes repaired. Walked until 1100 hrs, our shoes giving us trouble, wire fixings cutting into our feet. Decided to stop and rest, heat terrific, had a little to eat and drink, made shelter of brush. 0630 hrs made our way to edge of Qattara Depression. Hard going down cliff-side, very steep and dangerous in parts, ruined shoes completely.

'*Seventeenth Day.* Started walking, hard going, shoes giving trouble, very hot, salt marsh, fairly weak. Marsh was all dried up, we were walking over salt crags which in appearance resemble waves 18 to 24 inches high. Unable to walk in between same, we were compelled to walk along tops, stepping from one to another. It was very hot. Food and water both getting low.

'*Eighteenth Day*. Made camp at 0900 hrs. Sleep almost impossible, partly because of exhaustion and mostly because of continual gnawing in stomachs and thoughts of food and cool drinks that we could not keep out of our minds. Towards dusk met three Bedouin driving camels, who made us two rounds of bread six/seven inches in circumference, called grassa. Although they gave us almost unbearable attacks of indigestion, devoured to last morsel. Tonight we came upon soft salt, tough walking – placing one foot down it would sink up to shin in soft mud, and having no foothold it was necessary immediately to place other foot in front of first to keep walking. Made no more than 15 miles a day through this.

'*Twentieth Day*. Last night our food gave out, despite rationing. Water very low, about two bottles full. Very weak, shoes just about off our feet. At night came upon five Bedouin driving about 70 camels. They gave us handful of dates and drink of salty water.

'*Twenty-First Day*. Attempting to walk a few miles during day, weather not being very hot. Came across two Bedouin grazing camels, took us into camp and fed us with rice and camel's milk diluted with water. Former tasted like macaroni and cheese, the latter though very strong was quite refreshing.

'*Twenty-Second Day*. Entered camp amidst very curious Arabs. Fed on dates, rice and oil, and drank salty water. Quite a ritual. Still very weak but recovered.

'*Twenty-Fourth Day*. (November 2). Arrived at salt lake at about 0400 hrs, mosquitoes unbearable. Hearing, and finally sighting what seemed to be a motor lorry from a nearby hill about 0800, we headed north and were finally picked up by an advanced armoured division about 5-10 miles north of El Maghra.'

Purely to illustrate the wide variegation in 'walk-back' tales, the first-hand account of Lieutenant D. A. H. Clarke, SAAF, a Mustang pilot with 112 Squadron in Italy in 1944, exemplifies the perils of operating among the mountains of Italy, in direct contrast to the pitiless desert. On 3 June 1944, flying Mustang FX792, GA-X:

'I was hit in the engine at the beginning of my bombing dive, and without bombing immediately pulled up and reported I'd been hit and was baling out. I then dropped my bombs on road at G.3165 and reckon I got a direct hit. I took off my flying helmet and opened the canopy and started turning the aircraft over and winding tail trim forward. I turned aircraft halfway round and found I couldn't get it around any further, so released stick and shot halfway out of the cockpit. I then climbed out the rest of the way and

Below: **Self-evident problems for DAF Kittyhawks and jeep in Italy 1944.**/*IWM*

Above: **Kittyhawk IV, loaded with three 500lb bombs, believed to be from 112 Sqn in Italy.**/*IWM*

started somersaulting, which I was unable to stop. After about ten seconds I pulled the ripcord and the 'chute opened, and after taking stock of myself found my flying boot and revolver were missing. I saw my aircraft crash and burst into flames in the hills nearby. I landed in a very rocky piece of ground, but fortunately without injury. I then released the parachute and ran about ten yards, stopped, waved to my No 1 indicating I was OK. By this time some Italians had gathered, seemed very pleased to see me, and carried on a conversation which was all one-sided. I took further stock of my possessions and found that my escape purse and Italian booklet were missing; they too had fallen out of my overalls during my aerobatics. I then distributed my parachute, Mae West etc, and a few cigarettes amongst the Ities and set off for high ground in an easterly direction, but found walking with one flying boot on one foot and a flying glove on the other *not* the best type of footwear for mountain climbing!

'After sliding down Mount Aurore and washing my feet, I met an Italian in uniform who gave me half a loaf of bread and some very bitter cheese which I didn't eat. Having been told that Fascists were in Vallepietri, I set out for Trevi where I intended sleeping, but on seeing eight-plus Huns' MT in the village did a smart about-turn to the hills. I reached an abandoned hut in the hills at 10pm and found it bloody cold sleeping in a pair of overalls on the floor. Next morning I set out to cross the Trevi road but heard MT coming and dived under the bridge while two half-tracks went over the top. Then I went on my way, crossing a river up to my waist (damn cold too) and then up the mountains again, using by now my second glove as a shoe, the first having worn out. Near Monabianca I met up with some Italian cave-dwellers, who persuaded me to spend the night with them. At about 4pm, as I was sleeping, a boy woke me telling me 'Tedesci' were coming. I went into the bush and seven more came down the valley, going north in a hurry. After they'd passed I continued with my sleep. I was called up twice before sunset because of Jerries going through. The Ities fed me there on brown bread, goat's milk and raw eggs.

'Next morning two Italians offered to guide me to our lines, as they thought Jerry had left these parts. On the way I captured a Jerry HQ of some nature, complete with Orderly Room, beds, tables, chairs, blankets, bicycles and ammunition all left in confusion. The Jerries I'd seen had been carrying light arms only. At this camp I lifted an Italian cavalry sword, previously lifted by Jerry. I also got myself a right boot. The guides helped themselves to the kit and bicycles left behind. I then set off down the road towards Guarcino carrying a white flag and a bayonet, inspecting MT, tanks, guns (a couple of 88mm) that had been bombed and strafed. Some had been burned out, others just blown off the road, and others completely riddled. Several German graves were by the roadside too. I passed quite a number of Indians (6th Div) who took no notice of me, but later got captured by a doctor and eight others pointing their guns at me. After making myself known, they gave me a cup of tea, something to eat, a cigarette, and transport back to Div HQ. I spent one night with them and they treated me very well indeed. Before returning to 112 Squadron [on 7 June] I had to go forward with them over my tracks to their position in the line, where they gave me a new outfit before leaving.'

The DAF's last special sortie of the war occurred on 21 March 1945, when a precision attack was ordered to be launched on Venice harbour. Group Captain George Westlake had only recently joined 239 Wing as its Wing Commander Flying;
'Our main task was interdiction – bridges, railways, trains, ships, gun positions, troops, jetties, barges, in fact almost anything in northern Italy and Yugoslavia. However, Venice was not a low-level raid but a full-blooded dive-bomb attack, using the whole of 239 Wing, plus the whole of the US 79th Group – the only time Venice was ever attacked because of its status as a protected city. We had such a tight bomb-line, with such strict orders that not a single bomb was to destroy any civilian houses or places of historical interest; that the C-in-C openly told us that if there was a cock-up, not only would he be sacked, but that the Air Officer Commanding, Senior Air Staff Officer, and myself as leader of the formation would also be bowler-hatted – hence the code-name Operation "Bowler" for this particular show.'

Thus, the Mustangs of 112, 260, 3 RAAF and 5 SAAF Squadrons, some acting in the flak suppression role, the Kittyhawks of 250 and 450 Squadrons, the three P-47 squadrons of the US 79th Fighter Group all went into the attack. As they came in to bomb, the Venetians crowded the roofs of their historic city to watch the spectacular free show. In the target harbour area a number of barges, a tanker, and a torpedo boat were set afire and sunk, while the *SS Otto Leonhardt* was severely damaged. Five large storage sheds were demolished, and nearly 200 feet of the west quay shattered. Only a single stray bomb actually fell on the town. Lieutenant B. A. Senior, SAAF, of 250 Squadron, who was flying as Westlake's No 2, was forced to bale out into the sea after his Kittyhawk was hit by flak. Almost before he hit the water an air-sea rescue Catalina flying boat landed alongside him – he was back at base soon after the last fighter-bomber landed. And no one got his bowler . . .

Below: **Royal visitor. HM King George VI studies 239 Wing target photos, Italy 1944.**/*Dr F. T. Pearce*

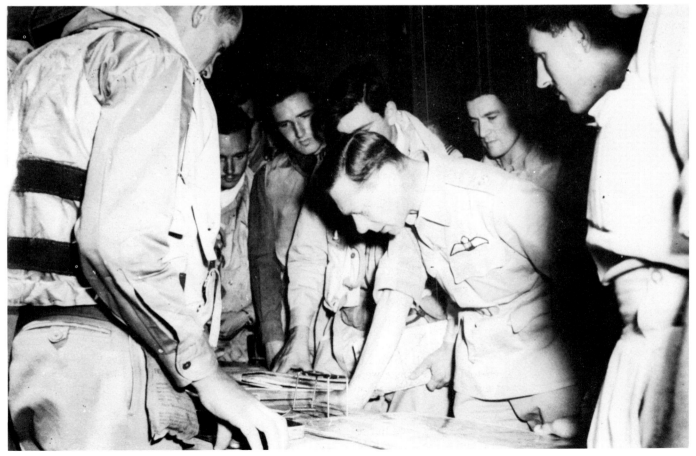

DAF, I presume?

Right: **This 'Jon' cartoon first appeared in** *Eighth Army News;* **epitomising the legendary 'individual' dress of most DAF men.**/*Courtesy J. A. Jones ('Jon')*

Below right: **Flt Lt O. V. Tracey DFC (left) of 274 Sqn, a New Zealander who served with 79 Sqn in the Battle of Britain; with the South African Lt Hoffe whom he rescued from the desert by 'pick-up' on 1 December 1941. Just seven days later Tracey was killed in action.**

Below: **AVM Arthur Coningham, AOC DAF from August 1941 to February 1943, seen here at LG 97 in September 1942.**/*F. J. Edwards*

"DESERT AIR FORCE—WE PRESUME, OLD MAN"

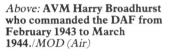

Above: **AVM Harry Broadhurst who commanded the DAF from February 1943 to March 1944./*MOD (Air)*

Below: **Top brass of 244 Wing, Italy, late 1943. From left: Sqn Ldr P. S. 'Stan' Turner (417 Sqn); Sqn Ldr P. H. Humphreys (92 Sqn); Wg Cdr W. G. G. Duncan-Smith (Wing Leader); Gp Capt C. B. F. Kingcombe (OC Wing); Sqn Ldr L. C. Wade (145 Sqn); Major M. S. Osler, SAAF (601 Sqn)./*IWM*

Above: 112 Sqn personnel at Fort Maddelena on 30 November 1941. From left: Sgt Leu; Neville Duke; Fg Off Soden; Fg Off 'Hank' Humphreys; Sqn Ldr D. G. H. Morello; Flt Lt Ambrose; Fg Off Dickenson; Sgt Burney; Fg Off Westenra; Fg Off Sabourin; Fg Off Bowker; Fg Off Bartle; Sgt 'Kit' Carson./*IWM*

Above right: Major J. E. Frost of 5 Sqn SAAF./*IWM*

Right: Three from 112 Sqn. Flt Lt D. F. Westenra, Flt Lt N. Duke DFC, and Flt Lt P. J. Humphreys. Note undone top buttons on all jackets – the unofficial mark of the fighter pilot then./*R. A. Brown.*

Below right: HM King George VI shaking hands with Lt-Col B. McKenzie DSO, DFC, third commander of 458 Sqn RAAF, though he was SAAF. It was the occasion when McKenzie obtained royal permission to retain his unmilitary side-whiskers . . . !

Right: Fg Off J. O. 'Tex' Gray in his 112 Sqn Kittyhawk, FL886, GA-K at Cutella, Italy circa February 1944. Tex, an American who joined the RCAF, was never officially posted to the unit, but scrounged a flight from Cairo to Italy and talked the local group captain into letting him stay with 112 to fight his 'own war' . . ./*R. A. Brown*

Below: Wg Cdr (later, Gp Capt) Billy Drake DSO, DFC who commanded 112 Sqn from May 1942 to January 1943. Seen here wearing his award of an American DFC./*IWM*

Above left: Major J. E. Parsonson DSO, DFC, OC 5 Sqn SAAF. Twice shot down and made prisoner, he escaped both times, only to be made prisoner again on 20 April 1943 when he was forced to ditch in the sea near Zembra Island./*IWM*

Above: Lt-Colonel L. A. Wilmot SAAF who commanded 239 Wing in Italy./*RNZAF*

Left: Wg Cdr John Bisdee DFC, ex-commander of 601 Sqn, who was appointed military governor of Lampedusa after its surrender.

Top: **Major G. J. Le Mesurier, OC 1 Sqn SAAF in mid-1942, with his Hurricane BG971, 'V'.**/*IWM*

Top centre: **Flt Sgt E. S. Doherty DFM, a New Zealander with 242 Sqn who claimed at least seven victories.**

Top right: **Sqn Ldr Lance Wade DSO, DFC who served with Nos 33 and 92 Sqns, then commanded 145 Sqn, claiming at least 26 combat victories. He was killed in a flying accident on 12 January 1944.**

Above: **Sgt R. J. Whittle DFM of 250 Sqn.**

Above right: **Wg Cdr Colin Gray DSO, DFC (centre) with his pilots who took part in the 'Junkers Party' off Messina on 25 July 1943.**/*Gp Capt C. F. Gray*

Right: **Gp Capt Brian Eaton RAAF, OC 239 Wing in Italy, cuts the Wing's 'third birthday' cake on 24 April 1945.**/*Dr F. T. Pearce*

Old Glory was there

The multi-national character of the Desert Air Force, which eventually included crews fron ten different countries, was probably the greatest factor in its overall successes. Men from England, Ireland, South Africa, Australia, France, Greece, and other nations mixed easily in the common cause, without rancour or more than health rivalry. Although principally a British Commonwealth organisation, the DAF was also to enjoy a valuable American contribution to its strength for a large part of its existence. Indeed, some of the first USAAF units to serve outside the USA against the western members of the Axis flew their initial operations with the DAF in North Africa.

American high command was never wholly keen on the Mediterranean as a major theatre of war, regarding it as something of a side-show and therefore a dilution of effort from the prime task of defeating Germany in western Europe. However, in view of Churchill's unshakeable view that invasion of Europe could not be considered before mid-1943 at the earliest, and when Rommel's Gazala offensive in May-June 1942 pushed British forces all the way back into Egypt; the US military command agreed, albeit reluctantly, to assist in clearing up the North African struggle once and for all, in order to prepare all further effort towards the ultimate goal of invading Europe.

An Anglo-American invasion of Morocco, Algeria and Tunisia, to attack Rommel's forces from the rear, went into immediate planning stages; but in the interim more immediate help for the Allies in Egypt was offered in the form of aerial reinforcement. In July 1942 the USAAF's 57th Fighter Group embarked on the aircraft carrier *USS Ranger* for transfer to Africa, while the 12th BG (Medium) prepared to fly across the south Atlantic as the first leg of a journey to Egypt. By early August both Groups were ensconsed in their new bases and working up for their baptism of fire. At that period a majority of the WDAF's air crews were wartime-trained men, with a leavening of experienced and long-service personnel mainly at flight or squadron commander levels; but in contrast the American crews, despite a total lack of combat experience, were thoroughly trained peace-time regular servicemen, and their flying skills and numerous logged flying hours were impressive, auguring well for their introduction to actual fighting.

The British, Australian and South African squadrons of the WDAF then were already flying Allison-engined versions of the Curtiss P-40 Kittyhawk, but the 57th FG brought with it P-40F Warhawks, powered by the licence-built Packard-Merlin; a better all-round variant which began to reach some RAF units before the year was out. The 12th BG was equipped with the B-25C Mitchell bomber, a type yet to see operational use in the western war zone but an aircraft which was to prove reliable and efficient.

Recognising their deficiencies in sheer combat experience, the American crews were eager to learn, and the new units were accordingly attached to WDAF units in the front line. While the 12th BG was attached in its entirety to 3 Wing, SAAF to fly alongside the South Africans' Bostons and Baltimores; one squadron from the 57th FG was attached to each of the RAF's Kittyhawk Wings – the 64th FS joining 233 Wing, and the 66th FS joining 239 Wing. These fighter pilots flew their first operational sorties on 8 August, while the US bombers undertook their initial missions just eight days later; though the latter were not the first USAAF aircraft to see action in the area because B-24 Liberators had already made several sorties with RAF Middle East, though not as part of the WDAF.

The American fighters registered their first claim on 14 August, when Lt Bill O'Neill of the 64th FS, flying one of six P-40Fs with a 260 Squadron Kittyhawk formation, claimed two Bf109s shot down before he was brought down in the sea. By September a third unit of the 57th FG, the 65th FS, had also joined 233 Wing. When the Alamein battle started in October the Americans had gained sufficient experience to fly as a group in their own right. As a tactic for the contemporary role of fighter-bombing, however, a three-squadron group was not ideal, and therefore in November the 57th FG was joined by the

RAF's 112 'Shark' Squadron, which flew in partnership with the 66th FS for the next three months.

Throughout October and November 1942 the US Warhawks enjoyed considerable success in combat, with a rapidly mounting tally of victories, although losses for the period also rose to rather high levels. The Mitchell bomber crews played a regular part in the overall bombing assaults, sending out tight formations of some 18 aircraft at a time to attack Rommel's troops and supply lines, during and after the Alamein battle. Meanwhile, in November, a second Group of P-40Fs, the 79th FG, reached Egypt, and initially one of its squadrons, the 85th FS, was attached to the 57th FG to gain experience. By the start of March 1943 this Group was also operating under its own aegis. Early in January 1943, however, a lack of adequate bombing targets led to two of the 12th BG's four squadrons being detached to Algeria to fly with the USAAF's 12th Air Force's B-25 units on the central Tunisian front.

By now the US 9th Air Force had been set up to administer all USAAF units in the Egyptian-Libyan zones, including heavy and medium bombers, fighters and transports; though for operations the medium bombers and the fighters remained under WDAF control. It was at this time that American strength within the WDAF reached its real peak, with a third P-40F unit, the 324th FG, in Egypt and about to despatch two of its squadrons to the front on attachment to the existing FGs, and another B-25 Group, the 340th, about to enter operations. Then, on 18 February 1943, came a reorganisation of the Allied air forces in the Mediterranean, including the formation of the North-West African Tactical Air Force with its three subordinate commands. The third of these was the Tactical Bomber Force to which, initially, all light and medium bomber units from the old WDAF, including the 12th BG and the 340th BG, were transferred. Though the newly-titled DAF would later recover its Boston and Baltimore squadrons, the American bomber units did not rejoin.

There still remained three US fighter

Above: **'Que Pasa' – a P-47 Thunderbolt of the 66th FS, 57th FG, flown by Lt Wayne S. Dodds.**/*W. S. Dodds*

Left: **P-47D 'Razorback' Thunderbolt of the 79th FG with RP tubes and jettisonable fuel pod, Italy late 1944.**/*Dr F. T. Pearce*

Groups within the DAF, alongside the force's RAF, RAAF and SAAF units. Air combat had by now become the prerogative of the Spitfire squadrons, while the Warhawks concentrated mostly on fighter-bombing. On 2 March the 57th FG and 79th FG, each with an additional squadron attached from the 324th FG, participated in the massive fighter-bomber assaults against the Tebaga Gap defences, in the face of the most intensive flak yet experienced in Africa.

The following months saw the Groups taking part in Operation 'Flax' patrols – seeking to intercept German transport aircraft formations shuttling between Sicily and Cape Bon, Tunisia. The greatest US successes in this form of operation was claimed by the Lockheed Lightning P-38-equipped units of XII Air Support Command, but the climax of such interceptions was reached during the evening of 18 April, when the 57th FG, with its attached 314th FS, met a vast formation of Junkers Ju52/3m transports off the African coast under a small fighter escort. In short order the Warhawks had a field day of

destruction in what has become known as the 'Palm Sunday Massacre'. No less than 75 Axis aircraft were claimed as shot down, for the loss of six P-40Fs. Typical of the many combat reports afterwards are those of two pilots from the 65th FS, Captain Roy Whittaker and Second Lieutenant Dick Hunziker. Whittaker's account reads in part; 'I attacked the Junkers from astern at full throttle and fired at two planes in the leading formation. The burst were short and the only effect I saw was pieces flying off the cabin of the second ship. I pulled away and circled right, then made a second attack. I fired two more burst into two more Ju52s – again in the leading formation. They both burst into flames. The second flew a little distance, then crashed into the water – I lost sight of the first and didn't see it hit. I then made a third pass and sent a good burst into the left of the formation, at another Junkers. As I pulled away it crashed into the water. By that time the Me109s were among us. As I pulled up to the left I saw a 109 dive through an element of four Warhawks and I tagged on his underside and gave him a long burst in the belly. He crashed into the sea from 1000 feet.'

Hunziker, on only his second combat mission, was highly excited as he sighted the sprawling Junkers' formation:

'On our first pass I was so excited that I started firing early. I could see the shots kicking up the water. Then they hit the tail of a six-engine plane* and crawled up the fuselage. This ship was near the front of the first Vee. As I went after it I realised I was being shot at from transports on both sides. It looked as though they were blinking red flashlights at me from the windows. The ship I was firing at hit the water in a great sheet of spray and then exploded. As I pulled away I could see figures struggling away from what was left of the plane. I then heard a voice yelling, "There's Me109s up here! C'mon up and help us!" I banged my throttle wide open and pulled back the stick and shot up to where I found a hell of a dogfight going on. I didn't even have time to flub around. As soon as I showed up an Me109

bounced me hard. I shook him and finally got on the tail of another fighters. As I was closing I noticed gold balls streaming past me on both sides. That meant another 109 had latched on my tail and was firing at me with his 20mm cannon. I evaded and came out over the shoreline where I hooked on to another fighters. I gave him a short burst which splashed into his nose. Pieces flew off the 109 and he nosed down steeply. I followed him down to the deck and saw him crash in a green field with a big splash of smoke and flame.'

With the conclusion of the campaign in Tunisia, some reorganisation was again made. The 57th FG and 79th FG reformed with the DAF, but the 324th FG was transferred to XII ASC. Though the DAF played little part in the air assault on the island of Pantelleria which followed shortly after, the two American Groups were involved, flying bomber escorts to the units of the Tactical Bomber Force. Later in June the two Groups accompanied the Kittyhawk Wings to Malta, from where they helped support the Eighth Army over the eastern side of the Sicily invasion landings. Moves to air strips on Sicily followed, from where they became much involved in interdiction missions against

*An error in identification, due to his inexperience.

Right: **Spitfire IX of the 31st FG.**/*G. R. McDowell*

Below: **Messerschmitt Me323 off Cape Bon on 30 July 1943, under attack from Wg Cdr W. Maydwell DSO, DFC in a 14 Sqn Martin Marauder.**/*IWM*

enemy shipping in the Straits of Messina. In early September support was given to the Eighth Army's landings in Calabria in the south of Italy, and by mid-month both Groups were established at airfields on the Italian mainland. By October they were based at fields in the Foggia complex, from where the 57th, in particular, flew a number of missions over southern Yugoslavia in support of Tito's partisans.

The 57th FG was to be the first Group in the Mediterranean to take the P-47D Thunderbolt into action; some early 'razor-back' models of this hefty fighter having reached the unit during November. These soon joined the P-40s on sorties over Italy and Yugoslavia, though it was to be several weeks before full re-equipment was completed. On 15 January 1944, however, the 79th FG, which had just begun receiving P-47s as well, left the DAF and flew to western Italy, along with several other DAF units, to add weight to the Anzio landings. And in March the DAF said farewell to its sole remaining American unit, when the 57th FG moved to Naples via Corsica for special interdiction duties over northern Italy.

In October 1944 the DAF was able to welcome back some of its 'Yanks' when the 79th FG returned, after service in the south of France. While glad to renew old friendships in the DAF, the American crews were not so enamoured of being back in 'sunny Italy' in winter. 'The reception in Italy was just what we dreaded,' noted the Group historian, 'Rain, mud and cold made up the receiving committee. The bivouac areas were true-to-life "Mudville" and the intermittent rain left the goo gooey. The airfield at Jesi had a concrete runway, but the dispersal areas were inches deep in mud.'

The 79th FG was to continue supporting the Eighth Army throughout that last winter of fighting and the following spring, being engaged in the later stages of the Gothic Line battle and the final victorious advance across the north Italian plains. Their unceasing bombing, rocket, and strafing attacks on German positions were highly appreciated by the army, as one message received from the commander of the 10th Infantry Brigade made clear; 'Please accept our grateful thanks and genuine admiration for the brilliant attacks by your rocket-firing Thunderbolts. The deadliness and accuracy of your attacks thrilled and stimulated all our boys to no ordinary degree. Come up and see us again just as soon as you can.' It was a fitting tribute to the DAF's 'American cousins' . . .

Below: **Spitfire V from the 52nd FG heavily damaged by flak undergoing repairs, February 1943.**/*USAF*

A Piece of cake

By early 1945 the campaign in Italy was reaching its final stages. Nevertheless, the DAF's activities both by day and by night continued at a high pitch of operational effort. The following first-hand account of a Baltimore 'reconnaissance' sortie by night is told by Warrant Officer Knight of 454 Squadron, RAAF of 253 Wing:

'Y-for-Yoke is standing in the dispersal close by, her dew-covered wings shining in the moonlight. Leaping from the truck we pull our parachutes and Mae Wests after us and dump them by the aircraft as the truck jerks into motion and hurtles down the taxi track. A fitter and a rigger are standing by and soon activity in and around the aircraft resembles six mice on a large lump of cheese. The fitter is hauling the tarpaulin covers from the engine; the rigger, sitting astride the nose, is wiping dew from the perspex with a chamois. "Cog" (the W/AG) and "Taffy" (the gunner) are in the back room stowing parachutes and

checking equipment. The nav, Max, calls up to the pilot, "Ready for bomb check, Mitch; all clear boom doors". Mitch, standing on the wing placing his 'chute in his cockpit, leans across and pulls a lever. "Ha-H-H-HA-A-A-A-A" . . . with a long heavy sigh the belly of the Balt swings down and out, revealing two rows of sleek yellow bombs. Standing in the bomb bays, the nav checks the fusing gear, then ducks out from under and clambers up his door-cum-ladder into the office, where the bomb selection gear is checked.

' "Load OK – Bomb doors closed", and "Whoosh" the doors swing shut and the belly of the aircraft is again a smooth, unbroken line. By 2130 all checking has been completed, the crew is aboard and the engines running. A rigger with two torches guides us out from the dispersal and gives the thumbs up as we turn down the taxi strip. Four hundred yards' taxying brings us to the end of the runway, where the pilot does his final cockpit drill and

Below: **454 Sqn armourers unloading the bomb wagon at dispersal.**

Above: **Baltimore F-Freddie of 454 Sqn with 61 ops already logged.**/*V. Cashmore*

tests his engines, then calls the Control Tower by R/T; "Hello Hillpath★ from Flippant Three-Five – Ready for immediate scramble – Over". "Flippant Three-Five from Hillpath – clear to go – Over". "Roger Hillpath; Three-Five Out." The night intruder lumbers forward, turns, and is soon thundering down the runway between the two rows of lights on the ground. At about 100mph she bounces once or twice and becomes airborne. The wheels fold back into the engine nacelles and the flarepath falls rapidly below and behind. A few minutes later we are over the flarepath again, at 4000 feet, and headed north for the Po river, our patrol area for tonight.

'A good moon is up and the coastline is clearly visible as it slides slowly backwards beneath us. On the way up a light on the sea is investigated but found to be a sea marker dropped by another aircraft. Soon the nav lights are switched off and the bombs fused and selected. Looking out to port we can see the artificial moonlight and the flashes and explosions of the 8th Army's artillery fire. Just north of this, over enemy territory, an occasional flare appears in the sky. The night

intruders are looking for enemy movement on the roads. Occasionally too, the red and white chameleon-tongues of tracer reach up from the ground trying to pull the intruders from the sky.

'As we pass Porto Garibaldi on the Comacchio Spit we ease away a little, for this is a definite hot spot. Altering course at Goro, we soon reach Taglio do Po and turn west along the river, beginning our patrol at 2211. We are to cover a 40-mile section of the Po until 2315. Passing Polesella, a noted hot spot, we are alert for any hostile action, for it was here one night that Jerry nearly claimed another aircraft destroyed – us! Stooging along we see a light switched off in a large building in a village. Noting this, we move on looking for better targets. The country 3000 feet below us looks dark and still; the only lights showing are fires dotted around the area, and from the sky flares are still dropping intermittently. About four miles on our port bow a flare lights up a sharp bend in the river. Mitch's voice comes over the intercom; "I think I see a bridge down there, Max. Should there be one there?" "No", replies the nav, "It's probably a pontoon affair – someone's bombing it now". Three streams of tracer slide up from the south bank almost converging at 4000 feet,

★ Hillpath was the call-sign of a PSP aerodrome at Cesenatico, near the beach, not far from Cervia where 239 Wing was based.

123

Right: **Going over – 454 Sqn Baltimores en route to target.**

Above: **Wg Cdr M. J. Moore, OC 454 Sqn from April to November 1944.**/*V. Cashmore*

Above right: **Sqn Ldr Vic Cashmore, RAAF of 113 and 454 Sqns.**/*RAAF*

and we see four bombs exploding in the river and on the bank quite close to the bridge. "Let's go in and have a *shufti* (look). If it's still in one piece we'll come back and bomb". "Right. Here we go. Keep your eye on the bridge, Cog, and see if there are any holes in it."

'Cog is over the open hatch in the rear of the aircraft and has a good view of anything directly below. We are over the bridge at 3000 feet and the old Balt is weaving like a bat. A single stream of tracer slides beneath us but is not very accurate. Satisfied the bridge is in good condition, we peel off and scream for the deck heading back up the river – but we'll be back. Finding nothing along the river, we turn again towards our bridge and as we approach a light blinks once near the centre. "See that light, Mitch?" The nav is kneeling over his bomb sight in the nose of the aircraft. "Yes, MT I think. The bridge is certainly in use. I'm turning in now", and the wing dips as we do a

diving turn onto the target. From the rear the W/AG's voice comes up, "Do you want me to toss out a flare, Max?" "No thanks, Cog, I'll use the moonpath – OK Mitch, hold her there." The plane levels out and the nav speaks again; "Height 2500 feet, Mitch?" . . . "Yep" . . . "Oke . . . left-left . . . steady . . . bomb doors open . . . damn! right ten degrees . . . hold it . . . bombing 1-2-3 . . . bomb doors closed . . . break left". As the aircraft makes its breakaway turn the invisible weight of the "G" presses down on us, and Taffy speaks from the turret, "A burst of light tracer well below". Cog reports on the bombing, "Overshot to the southern bank – one on the bank, one near the road, one on a house." "OK. Thanks, Cog" the nav replies and thinks, "Not good but better luck next time – *yimkin* (perhaps)."

'Last night we were photographing Francolino where Jerry was suspected to be crossing, so we circle here a few times dropping flares from 2000 feet. Satisfied there are no pontoons or ferries crossing the river, we stooge off. Activity was also expected near Polesella tonight, so we circle there doing bags of evasive action and firing off illuminating cartridges. These light a section of the ground brilliantly for ten seconds each, but no movement or MT seen. "Let's go down a bit, Mitch, and have a *shufti* around the roads between the Po and the Adige." Cog is becoming restless. "Right. Going down". At something like 500 feet our descent is checked and we go weaving and turning around roads and canals. "MT below us" – Cog has sighted a target. Turning, we fly back along the road and make three or four passes over a large truck parked by the roadside. Cog is strafing with his two belly guns and the smell of cordite fills the aircraft. We have only ten minutes left on patrol and we must dump our bombs on something, so we leave the truck and continue the search. During those few short minutes we see an exhibition of really good shooting but did not like it one little bit – our aircraft was the clay pigeon.

'At 500 feet we flew over the moonlit countryside, the nav's head thrust as far forward into the perspex nose as possible for better vision, the pilot concentrating on his flying and at the same time looking for MT, the W/AG crouched over his open hatch, and Taffy constantly turning his turret searching for enemy fighters. From the bank of a canal, without warning, a long thin yellow tongue of tracer licks out trying to caress old Y-Yoke. The nav's head shoots back into the body of the aircraft like a scared tortoise. Mitch dives the aircraft to starboard and levels out quick – you can't dive far when you start from 500 feet. That thin yellow line stays just over the turret, and weave as we did we couldn't lose it. We are clipping along at a smart 220mph some 50 feet above the deck when the gun, probably a 20mm, finally lost us and ceased firing. It was just after this that we all start breathing again. "Yah, missed me!" says Mitch, and his breath comes in uneven pants through the microphone.

'Max suddenly realises that he is still alive after all and speaks up, "We still have these bombs on and it's almost time we went home. I think we'd better go down to the river. We're sure to find something there". "What height?" the pilot wants to know as he turns south. "About four thou". "Four thousand it is" and we start climbing. Just as we turn along the river a pontoon bridge is silhouetted in the moonpath. "Target 40 degrees port. Start turning." The navigator is over his bomb sight again and his eyes keep the bridge in sight as his fingers feel along the bomb switches and select those required. "Are you going for that bridge?" – the pilot sighted it too. "That's right. Weave right, then back again . . . OK steady there . . . bomb doors open . . . left-left . . . hold it . . . bombing 1-2-3 . . . bomb doors closed, break left." The bombs hurl up geysers of water about fifty yards east of the bridge. Not good enough. The nav speaks again, "Your course 160 degrees – more or less." "Are we going home now?", comes a query from the turret. "Yes, Taff", says Mitch, "We're pointing right at it, more or less". "Goodie, goodie" says Taff.

'We are late leaving patrol for it's now 2325, so we try to send an ETA to base by W/T but cannot get through. We fly down over the lake watching the terrific 8th Army barrage. Looking back over enemy territory fires can be seen scattered everywhere. Flares and bombs are still going down and tracer is still coming up. It will be like that all night. In the morning the fighter and daylight formation bombers will continue the harassing and pounding. Reaching the south shore of the lake we alter course and head down towards base. At 2345 we're calling the Control Tower.

' "Hello Hillpath, this is Flippant Three-Five. Landing instructions please. Over". "Hello Flippant Three-Five from Hillpath. You're No.1 and clear to land. Over". "Roger Hillpath. Three-Five Out." We complete the circuit of the 'drome and come in. Safety harnesses are fastened and we settle back into our seats as the aircraft is aimed as though to dive into the ground just short of the flarepath. As usual though, we level out, sink, bump once, and we are rushing down a lane between two rows of lights at 100mph. The nav enters in his log "Landed Base 2348", as we taxi back to dispersal. The aircraft is parked, engines stopped, and we clamber out among the ever-waiting ground crew. "How was the trip, Mitch?" one of them asks. "A piece of cake" is the reply . . .'

Below: **Letting go – 454 Sqn's Baltimores releasing their loads amongst the usual flurry of flak bursts.**/*V. Cashmore*

Above: **An attack by 24 Baltimores from 454 Sqn against Fiume on 5 November 1944.**/*V. Cashmore*

Right: **454 Squadron Baltimore 'X-X-Ray' and its crew. The ops log shows 56 sorties completed.**

Epitaph

'Friend' or 'Foe' – all died for their homeland. Above, the Allies' cemetery at Tobruk; and (left) a Macchi 200's fuselage forms part of an Italian station grave at El Adem.

Bibliography

Remarkably few books have been published which deal with the Desert Air Force *per se*, though a wealth of literature can be found covering all or parts of the aerial warfare throughout the Middle East theatres during the years 1939-45. The following selection of titles are commended to those readers wishing to delve more deeply into the history of the DAF itself, and the much broader background against which the DAF should be considered during its relatively brief existence as an individual fighting formation.

The Desert Air Force; R. Owen; Hutchinson, 1948.
Middle East, 1940-42; P. Guedalla: Hodder & Stoughton, 1944.
Imshi; A. Myers; W. H. Allen, 1943.
Libyan Log; E. G. Ogilivie; Oliver & Boyd, 1943.
They Flew through Sand; G. W. Houghton; R. Schindler, Cairo, 1942.
Wings over Olympus; T. Wisdom; Allen & Unwin, 1942.
Triumph over Tunisia; T. Wisdom; Allen & Unwin, 1944.
Near East; C. Beaton; Batsford, 1943.
Malta Spitfire; G. Beurling/L Roberts; OUP Toronto, 1943.
Spitfires over Malta; R. Hesselyn/P. Brennan; Jarrolds, 1944.
Briefed to Attack; H. P. Lloyd; Hodder & Stoughton, 1949.
Tattered Battlements; H. Johnson; P. Davies, 1943.
Mediterranean Airpower; A. W. F. Glenn; Conrad Press, 1944.
RAF Middle East Review, 1942-45; Crown Copyright.
RAF Middle East; HMSO, 1945.
The Air Battle of Malta; HMSO, 1944.

80 Squadron; J. H. Schultz; 1945.
112 Squadron History; R. A. Brown, 1959.
Desert Squadron (272 Sqn); V. Houart; Souvenir Press, 1959.
Camera at War; H. Hensser; Jarrolds, 1945.
Paiforce; HMSO, 1948.
Escape to Live; E. Howell; Longmans, Green & Co; 1947.
Faith, Hope and Charity; K. Poolman; W. Kimber, 1954.
One Man's Window; D. Barnham; W. Kimber, 1956.
Pattle; E. C. R. Baker; W. Kimber, 1965.
The Unseen Eye; G. Millington; Gibbs & Phillips, 1961.
War in the Aegean; P. Smith/E. Walker; W. Kimber, 1974.
We Find and Destroy; P. Alexander; 458 Sqn Council, 1959.
Per noctem per diem; Tucker/MacGregor; 24 Sqn Album Committee, 1961.
Theirs is the Glory; S. McCreath; Widdicombe & Ogden.
3 Squadron at War; J. Watson/L. Jones; 3 Sqn Assn, 1959.
Wellington Wings; R. Chappell; W. Kimber, 1980.
Fighters over the Desert; C. Shores/H. Ring; N. Spearman, 1969.
Fighters over Tunisia; C. Shores/H. Ring/W. Hess; N. Spearman, 1975.
Pictorial history of the Mediterranean Air War, 3 Vols; C. F. Shores; Ian Allan, 1972-74.
Royal Air Force, 1939-45, 3 Vols; Richards/Saunders; HMSO, 1953-54.
RCAF Overseas, 3 Vols; OUP, 1946-47.
RNZAF Official History, 3 Vols; H. L. Thompson; War History Branch, NZ, 1953.
RAAF Official History, 4 Vols; Australian War Memorial, 1954.
SAAF History, 3 Vols; Brown/Martin/Orpen; Purnell, 1970-77